JACK LEMMON

JACK LEMMON

A Pyramid Illustrated History of the Movies

**by
WILL HOLTZMAN**

General Editor: **TED SENNETT**

**PUBLICATIONS
NEW YORK**

JACK LEMMON
A Pyramid History of the Movies

A PYRAMID BOOK

Copyright © 1977 by Pyramid Communications, Inc.

All rights reserved. No part of this publication may be reproduced or transmitted in any form or by any means, electronic or mechanical, including photocopy, recording, or any information storage and retrieval system, without permission in writing from the publisher.

Pyramid edition published April 1977

Library of Congress Catalog Card Number: 77-73159

Printed in the United States of America

Pyramid Books are published by Pyramid Publications (Harcourt Brace Jovanovich, Inc.). Its trademarks, consisting of the word "Pyramid" and the portrayal of a pyramid, are registered in the United States Patent Office.

PYRAMID PUBLICATIONS
(Harcourt Brace Jovanovich, Inc.)
757 Third Avenue, New York, N.Y. 10017

(graphic design by Anthony Basile)

ACKNOWLEDGMENTS

First thanks, as always, to my family and friends who make it all worthwhile.

I wish to acknowledge the assistance of Monty Arnold and the staff of the Theatre Research Collection at the Lincoln Center Library, and Barbara Humphrys and her colleagues at the Motion Picture Section of the Library of Congress.

Very special thanks to Rhonda Bloom for her friendship and generosity. Her taste in film is only exceeded by her taste in jazz.

My gratitude to Mark Frost, Bill Pearson, and Sue Holtzman for shelter from the storm, and to fellow travelers J. T. Spaulding, Phil Marlowe, and Dwayne Doberman.

I wish also to acknowledge Don Widener, whose extensive interviews with Jack Lemmon have been an invaluable source.

I am grateful to my editor, Ted Sennett, and especially to my good, good friend, Jeanine Basinger, for continued confidence and support.

Final thanks to Sylvia Shepard and Pearl, without whose love, good sense, and patience, this book would not have been possible.

Photographs: Jerry Vermilye, The Memory Shop, Movie Star News, CBS Photo Archives, and the companies that produced and distributed the films of Jack Lemmon

CONTENTS

Without Greasepaint	11
The Lemmon With Appeal	17
Pulver-ized	31
Jack's Dilemma	49
Wild, Wilder, Wildest	65
Good Neighbor Jack	97
Vintage Lemmon	115
Introducing Jack Lemmon	145
Bibliography	149
The Films of Jack Lemmon	151
Index	155

MY SISTER EILEEN (1955). As Bob Baker

The thirties may have been the decade of the bust, but the fifties was the decade of the breast, and Jack Lemmon appeared opposite some of the best in the business. That alone would have made him a baggy-pants buffoon. What made him a star was his ability to survive America's mixed bag of post-war fetishes. What makes him an actor is his ability to survive his stardom.

The talent begins with the face. It is a clown's face—oblong, large, blank, with a timid shovel jaw. The small eyes are frantic, the eyebrows thickly operatic, the nose handsome but intrusive, the mouth a thin line of expression sagging to a slight frown at either side. It is an innocent face, almost boyish, but shaded by a dense beard that he wears like a mask. In medium shot, the face is placid bordering on bland, but in close-up, the features become mobile. The mouth curls and twitches, the eyes dart and twinkle, the nose probes and wrinkles.

The body is just the face in limbs. It has the same kinetic undercurrent, even in repose. It is compact, rabbit quick, though oddly inelastic, and round shoulders cramp the 5' 11" stature. Like Cagney, the center of gravity is just forward of the balls of the feet, and the elbows seem hinged at a nearly waistless torso. Unlike Cagney, Lemmon's is a posture of resignation and retreat, not defiance. The visual Lemmon speaks before the actor utters a word.

WITHOUT GREASEPAINT

"I don't want you to think that I'm stuffy or uptight. I'm considered a pretty groovy cat. You know, tuned in."—as Wendell Armbruster in *Avanti*, 1972

There are those who see Lemmon as a curious star composite. A face like Lew Ayres. The adenoidal voice of Robert Walker. The strutting walk of Cagney. The sputtering speech of Billy Gilbert. The huckster twang of Roscoe Karns. The physical comic facility of Cary Grant in miniature. The singing voice of a dancer and the dancing flair of a singer. The list rambles on with similar partial truths that offer no real clue to the man. What he really is, is Jack Lemmon, all wrapped up into one. But the wrapping was no easy matter.

Lemmon served his acting apprenticeship in television, when the medium was still alive and kicking. His ready versatility was given wide play, but his greatest commercial success was in light leading roles and as a comic actor. Commerce was what Hollywood had in mind when it snatched him from the jaws of television, and Lemmon was automatically typed as a comic character actor with potential as a lead. That translated easily into antic romance, supporting work, and musicals, which is precisely where his growth was stunted. Versatility had become a vice.

It took the prophetic shrewdness of Billy Wilder to see Lemmon's innate virtuosity. On little more than a hunch, the director rescued the actor from the misery of misuse, and hastily poured him into such typically pungent Wilder potions as *Some Like it Hot* and *The Apartment*. The talents meshed instantly, and Wilder and Lemmon struck a rare, fluent cinematic rapport to rival that of Howard Hawks and Cary Grant.

The breakthrough was not without setbacks. Lesser directorial talents continued to squander Lemmon on whatever property was at hand, leading to such popular atrocities as *Under the Yum Yum Tree* and *How to Murder Your Wife*. But performing in motion picture pulp, however glib or glossy, is the way actors come to personify their times, and Lemmon was no exception. In the late fifties and early sixties, the underlying concern of films, comic and dramatic, was the loss of human contact in an antiseptic, mechanized America. A peculiar symptom of this anxiety was an obsession with the physical woman, specifically the breast. Lemmon was passed from Judy Holliday, to Rita Hayworth, to Kim Novak, to Marilyn Monroe, to Shirley MacLaine, to Carol Lynley, to Virna Lisi, and emerged nearly smothered and much the worse for the wear. Busty as the company was, it had none of the mystery, sass, or sensuality of the thirties femme fatale, nothing like the smoldering sexuality necessary to thaw Cold War man. For the most part, their ample presence was anatomical, ironically, almost mechanical. And Lemmon was left to play stooge to America's neurosis.

Even after movies moved to the suburbs with *Good Neighbor Sam*, Lemmon was still made to pose as a schnook beside the fixtures of this new environment—pushy office executives, nerve-jangling children and pets, and meddlesome neighbors. Later, when movies moved back to the city and turned comically sinister at the hand of Neil Simon, Lemmon was again saddled with the weight of society's sins—municipal strikes, muggers, and more meddlesome neighbors. It's a wonder the Lemmon persona wasn't wholly straightjacketed and bundled off to a padded room, as it was briefly in *Days of Wine and Roses*.

For all of this, Lemmon maximized what few good roles fell his way, and, scrapping inch by inch, he slowly cross-stitched an ongoing character fabric. Comedy became his forte, but not his limit. In

GOOD NEIGHBOR SAM (1964). As Sam Bissel

SAVE THE TIGER (1973). As Harry Stoner

fact, it was an uncanny sense of comic timing that helped him, at length, to ripen into a dramatic actor of the highest caliber. After all, as Lemmon is quick to point out, comedy is just dry tears.

That's not to say his dramatic work is maudlin or weepy, but simply that it is an exquisite counterpart of his comedy, the clown without greasepaint. Thinly masked, Lemmon's mental workings seem virtually to simulate the movement of film through a camera, as if he is able to hear the sound of stock on the sprockets. He knows every beat, but does not play the meter to monotony. He paces, counterpoints, and pauses, but like a fine jazz pianist, he never loses the rhythm. He can even stammer or stumble unerringly on cue. His impeccable timing is his salvation; it lends cohesiveness and credibility to even the most fractured dialogue, character, or film.

But Lemmon's control is modestly underplayed, at times to perfection. His submerged balance anchors an outward skittishness. That tension of opposites is what permits Lemmon his basic comic skill, and yet prevents him from being basically a comedian. He can be a clown in the fullest sense, capable of pratfalls and pathos, as well as a compelling dramatic actor.

As clown and actor, Jack Lemmon engulfs his own commanding technique, leaving a subtle residue of realism which is the key to his vulnerability. He is a dazzling welterweight who bobs and weaves and jabs, then takes a knockout punch on the nose. Beyond a doubt, Lemmon's characters have taken more physical and psychological lumps than any of modern popular film. He is the premier underdog of our time.

Yet, on the surface of it, Lemmon's image is a paradox, both fixed and timeless. He is undeniably an artifact of contemporary America, but his style is agelessly pantomimic and fluid. If his repertoire refuses to bend to period or adventure, it is masterfully flexible, even classic, within its scope. No single category contains Jack Lemmon, except to say that he is, above all, an actor.

Or, as Billy Wilder indelicately concluded, "Lemmon had to be an actor. I doubt he could have done anything else, except play piano in a whorehouse."

On a frostbitten mid-December morning in 1953, a tidy but taut young actor skittered into the mid-Manhattan office of Bill Doll and Company. He was handed the customary pre-production questionnaire. It began by asking indifferently, *What was your first Broadway play?* The actor uncoiled a bit, chuckled to himself, and hastily penciled in the margin, "This one." As an afterthought, he leaned forward and sketched a dime-size moon face with broad grin and bashful eyes.

The balance of the questionnaire makes a handy personal history. *Name* "Jack Lemmon," John Uhler Lemmon III, to be exact. *Born* "1925" on the 8th of February. *Place of birth* "Boston, Massachusetts," actually Newton, prematurely in the elevator of the Newton-Wellesley Hospital—fragile, plug-headed, and acutely jaundiced, what else with a name like Lemmon? Little wonder that he was an only child.

Father "John Uhler Lemmon Jr." A former naval officer become bakery executive. First employed with Read Machinery, a bakery equipment outfit, then with Hathaway Bakery Company. Currently head of sales with the Doughnut Corporation of America. Dignified, dapper, shrewd. A Catholic by birth and practice. An amateur hoofer and songster with little aptitude for either.

THE LEMMON WITH APPEAL

"Hark, a pistol shot!"—as a walk-on in *Gold in Them Thar Hills*, 1929

Mother "Mildred LaRue Noel Lemmon." Millie, a dynamic, outgoing brunette, one of eleven immediate Noels, a prominent Maryland family and prosperous government contractor. A Baptist by birth and a bridge player by practice. Witty, urbane, and devoutly gregarious.

Your first professional role "*Gold in Them Thar Hills*." At age four, sickly but game, Jack made his stage debut as a walk-on in a charity show melodrama featuring his folks. He waddled onstage, planted himself squarely, and declared, "Hark, a pistol shot!" It didn't take. Jack preferred *Popular Mechanics* to popular theatrics; that, and conspiring with neighbor Brooks Slocum in a prankish reign of terror on the otherwise tranquil, tree-lined proximity of Newton's well-to-do Ivanhoe Street.

Education "Harvard, A.B." An instance where the credential scarcely speaks for itself. From his dread boyhood summers at Camp Mitigwa on Maine's Rangely Lake, where, apparently inspired by the locale, Jack proved himself a bedwetter extraordinaire, he seemed inevitably to be the center of attention. Better the source of amusement than the butt of it, Jack gradually defined himself within groups as the resident showman. His shyness and insecurity seemed to invert in this personality and, if hardly the village idiot, neither did he pose any threat to its intelligentsia. Comradeship became the prevailing theme at the expense of scholarship, and Jack's academic record became a stockpile of "D"s.

Between tonsillectomies and adenoid procedures (three of one, five of the other) and despite a generous sprinkling of measles, mumps, and rheumatic fever, Jack, aged nine, found time to enroll at the private Rivers Country Day School in neighboring Brookline. School wasn't much but it was a welcome relief from recent homefront stress, where the marriage of John and Millie had fallen on hard times. Four years did nothing to mend the rift, and by the time Jack was packed off to Andover Academy north of Boston, the parental tension had only slackened through companionate arrangements. For the dismayed young Jack, separate bedrooms was a riddle he'd sooner not have solved.

A spare, leery Lemmon hung up his coat in Williams Residence Hall and proceeded to make his mark at Andover as, of all things, an athlete. He had taken up distance running therapeutically to offset his general anemia and surprised everyone, especially himself, by developing into a top cross-country man. "The Boston Bullet," self-proclaimed, was a title he willingly renounced when he began to suspect his coach of a certain malign neglect. But there were other outlets.

The piano, for one. Jack, self-taught and without fail his own best audience, became a "noodler," a description which locates him somewhere between Tin Pan Alley and the Philharmonic. As his then close companion, Eddie Jordan, construed it, "That piano was his security blanket," right down to Jack's own moth-eaten melodies. There was more to this performing than mere musical refuge. Jack was conducting an elective course of his own down at the Old Howard Burlesque House, one of those hallowed rites of passage for male adolescents. But Jack was little teased by the strippers, certainly more pleased by the baggy pants comics who, amid tassels and G-strings, cooked up a sumptuous smorgasbord of those musty jokes and routines that are burlesque's stock-in-trade.

Andover being one of those select sanctuaries of eastern elitism, the start of the Second World War had little impact on Jack and his schoolmates. If nothing else, the ivory tower was providing a much needed shelter for Jack's growth. He cultivated personal interests, banished once and for all his poor health, and became more relaxed socially. Family anxiety eased as well, as John and Millie reconciled themselves to platonic terms, and, by the summer of Jack's junior year, the family was happily ensconced for the season on Lake Winnepesaukee in Wolfboro, New Hampshire. Jack became an avid fisherman, chummed around with his spunky neighbor Estelle Parsons, and gingerly set about extending his education into the field of carnal knowledge—as usual, he was mostly coming up with "D"s.

Jack returned to Andover that fall and graduated the following spring—but only just. The summer of '43 was spent as a stagehand and apprentice with the Marblehead Players, a fine summer stock troupe in a prosperous Massachusetts shore area, a convenient hour north of Boston. Estelle joined Jack, and life might have taken a temporary carefree turn had not his parents' marriage taken a final turn for the worse. John and Millie separated permanently and, to all reports, amicably. He took a room at the Sheraton, while she became something of a fixture at the Ritz-Carlton cocktail lounge.

Despite his lackluster stint at Andover, Jack wriggled into Harvard on the Navy's accelerated V-12 ROTC program. The young man who confidently hung up his coat at Eliot House that September was a far cry from the anxiety-ridden runt who checked into Andover four years earlier. Jack had broadened at the shoulders and stretched from his former rodent stature to a towering 5'11". His face had taken on a handsome angularity, and he was ready to take Harvard by storm, socially that is—his classroom performance remained a mere drizzle. A war sciences major by regulation, he pursued a dramatic arts minor by habituation.

The seed that was peculiarly Lemmon flourished. A supercharged man about campus, he became vice president of the Dramatic Club and the marginally bluenosed Delphic Club. He landed the role of Old Mahon in Maude DeWolfe Howe's staging of Synge's *The Playboy of the Western World*, billing himself as Timothy Orange in order to sidestep the sanctions of academic probation. Maintaining the fruit motif, he defeated an opponent named Appel to become president of Harvard's exclusive Hasty Pudding Club. Jack was now a certified extrovert.

In what can only be considered the crowning achievement of his long academic siege, Jack careened through his final exams, compiling the lowest marks of any officer ever commissioned by the Navy ROTC. In the wake of his accomplishment, he was summoned by the class dean, who read over the grave of Jack's monumental under-

achievement, and somberly intoned the following epitaph, "My boy, I don't see how you will ever amount to anything."

The questionnaire went on to ask about *War Activities*. "Ensign, United States Navy, communications officer aboard the *U.S.S. Lake Champlain*." In a stroke of luck for the allied war effort, Ensign Lemmon was commissioned well after V-E day and shortly before V-J day. There was little damage that could be done to the favorable fortunes of war, and that little he very nearly did.

The 888-foot, 24,000-ton carrier was only slightly smaller than Jack's home town of Newton. Although the young ensign's seafaring experience had not gone beyond a rowboat on Lake Winnepesaukee, he was dispatched to the *Champlain*, then at anchor in Norfolk, Virginia, and assigned to communications, about which he knew nothing. (On a good day, he might be able to spell "semaphore.") The carrier got under way en route to Newport News, Virginia for a transport assignment. The massive ship was no sooner out of port when a crippled tanker appeared, signalling frantically and closing on the *Champlain* with deadly speed.

Ensign Lemmon was called to the bridge and ordered to interpret the signals. He wouldn't have known a coded S.O.S. from a halibut in distress, but he nervously blurted out the first nautical term that jumped into his head. It happened to be the right one, and a collision was narrowly averted. The valiant effort won Lemmon a commendation, and, after logging a full two hours and twenty-two minutes at sea, he was made a desk jockey at the Navy decoding section in Washington D.C. From there, he was reassigned to the motor pool at the Fargo Building in Boston, and closed out his Naval career answering phones with, "Lemmon —jeeps."

Theatrical Work "Summer stock." Discharged from the Navy in the summer of 1946, Jack joined the North Shore Players in Beverly, Massachusetts. After a time, he landed a part as a walk-on in *Angel Street*, and, with bolstered confidence, auditioned for the part of Milner, the third lead in John Van Druten's *Young Woodley*. Child star Roddy McDowall was imported from Hollywood for the lead, and the scramble for the remaining parts was fierce now that the play was a cinch to win critical notice. Sporting a fog-thick British accent and uncharacteristic brashness, Jack was picked to play Milner. As the show went into performance, young Lemmon realized for the first time that he had found his calling. He was good, and he knew it.

Returning to Harvard in the fall for some scholastic odds and ends, Jack wangled a degree by December, and, breathing a sigh of relief, washed his hands of academics once and for all.

With theater as his chosen temple, Jack groomed himself for a pilgrimage to its Mecca, otherwise known as Manhattan. Accepting his father's blessings and backing (to the tune of $300), he boarded the morning train to New York and, by his own account, comported himself like anything but the master of melody and stagecraft he was sure to become: "I was grinning like a horse's ass because I was so thrilled, so filled with excitement. I was going to be the next Gershwin and I was going to save the American theater."

There were no brass bands waiting at Grand Central Station, just the usual complement of winos and hopheads. Figuring that the best location for this miracle-cure Lemmon was the very pulse of the ailing entertainment world, Jack took a room at a dive on 44th Street and Broadway, at three dollars a day. His loan started ticking off one per cent per diem. In short order, Jack launched successive assaults on the front offices of agents and producers, never penetrating beyond the reception desk. Thwarted time and again, he watched his funds evaporate at an alarming rate. He may have arrived on Broadway, but obviously going there was not getting there.

His morale sinking proportionately with his resources, Jack was heartened to bump into an old Winnepesaukee neighbor, Maury Shea, who owned a chain of movie theaters in town, and, more to the point for Jack, kept an apartment on the Upper East Side that had an achingly unoccupied sofa. Maury offered and Jack snapped it up, content to fall back from his foiled frontal assault on show business.

Prospects did not improve from this uptown bivouac and rather than outlive his welcome for what now promised to be a grinding uphill battle, Jack thanked Maury for his generosity, cast a last fond glance at the couch, and muttered something about an apartment opportunity he could hardly pass up. Perhaps he meant hardly *walk* up, since he moved to the fourth floor of a rooming house where the landlady, an autocratic Mrs. Martinelli, whittled a little pocket money from her actor residents by playing temperamental answering service to the first floor telephone. Jack did not care for his landlady or her racket, but the rent was an irresistible $1.75 per week. With the occasional free dinners he would get on his father's frequent business trips to town, plus the tens and twenties that would magically appear in his coat pocket after dessert, Jack was getting by.

With Ida Lupino in "Marriageable Male" on Ford All-Star Theatre, February 25, 1954

Still, his theatrical agent rounds only had him going in circles, so Jack tried some self-promotion and teamed with an acquaintance, Mitzi Mandelbaum, in an act designed for the Catskills resort circuit. The act shortcircuited for want of finance, and the closest Jack got to the Borscht Belt was Isaac Gellis's delicatessen, located one floor below the coldwater flat he had since taken on Delancey Street. At $2.50 a week, Jack was coming up in class but down in outlay by sharing the apartment with an old Harvard buddy, Andy McCullough. It took another Harvard connection to really get Jack on his feet.

Strolling back from an evening visit at Maury Shea's, Jack lingered outside the Old Knickerbocker Music Hall on the corner of 54th and Second Avenue and caught sight of a familiar face from college, Paul Killiam. It turned out that Killiam was operating the place as a joint venture. Jack took one look around and agreed with the first half of the description. When customers wanted food, you waited tables. When they wanted entertainment, you entertained. And on those rare nights when there was a profit, you got paid. For Jack, it was the best offer yet—the only offer. He took it.

The Old Knick was a blessing in disguise. A quaint anachronism, it was a last vestige of vaudeville, a place where performers could drop in, do a monologue, a dramatic vignette, or an old-fashioned buck and wing, get hooted off the stage, and come back the next night for another whack. In short, it was a place where you could bomb and live to bomb again, just the place for Lemmon. When he wasn't waiting tables or washing dishes, he put on a straw boater and acted as master of ceremonies and accompanist, serving up a brand of running patter that harked back to the Old Howard days. The operation was not strictly amateur. There were a few established actors who continued to trod the boards of the Old Knick, Jack Albertson chief among them.

Jack Lemmon believed his lean times were behind him, but John Lemmon was less convinced and arranged a transfer to New York, took an apartment uptown, and from this perch made sure that the young thespian kept a roof over his head and continued to eat with moderate regularity. But if the Old Knick was attending to Jack's necessities, it didn't offer much of a springboard into serious drama. Still combing the front offices and trade journals for that all-important entrée, Jack got wind of an upcoming production of Tolstoy's *The Power of Darkness*, to be directed by the distinguished drama coach, Uta Hagen. He whisked over and read for the part of Nikita, made the callbacks, and got the part.

With Lillian Gish and Raymond Massey at a rehearsal of "The Day Lincoln Was Shot," presented on Ford Star Jubilee, February 11, 1956

From vaudeville to Tolstoy in a twinkling, though given Jack's background, it wasn't exactly Jolson singing *Pagliacci*.

Cynthia Stone, an astute, personable young actress, was cast opposite Jack as Marina, and the play went into rehearsal. It opened several weeks later at the Ethnological Dance Studio with the program listing a John Uhler as Nikita. Jack was not about to tempt fate with "Lemmon" his first time out in New York, and, however dubious the reasoning, the result was fine. *The Power of Darkness* was warmly received and Hagen thought that the young man with the elusive last name just might be going places. The only place he was going after the opening was to dinner with Millie, who had come to town specially to see her son's New York debut. They were joined by Cynthia, who in recent weeks had become Jack's constant companion.

Good summers seemed to come in even numbers, and 1948 complied. On the recommendation of Jack Albertson, Don Dickenson, the director of the Hayloft Theatre in Allentown, Pennsylvania, signed Lemmon to summer stock. Jack was well served by his hybrid theatrical background, and went on to win notice in everything from melodrama to Oscar Wilde. He ranged through *The Drunkard, Three Men on a Horse, Dark of the Moon,* *John Loves Mary*, and *Lady Windermere's Fan*, and was the season's matchless show stopper as a novice inebriate in *Apron Strings*. Jack was not without grounds for a guarded optimism about the future. But then, Allentown was not New York, and New York was what lurked around the corner.

The questionnaire was curious about *Radio Work*. Had he chosen to reply, Jack might have mentioned that the best he could swing after his halcyon days at the Hayloft was a supporting role in an NBC radio soap opera. Three times a week, Jack shot over to Rockefeller Center, took the elevator to *The Brighter Day* studio, and became "Bruce" at $25 a throw. That soon led to the part of young "Butch Brent" on another daytime weeper, *Road of Life*, all of which was fast leading nowhere. Jack was not a recital actor and his previous summer's experience had done more to nurture his physical acting instincts than his voice. Deprived of his newfound strength, Jack was prone to nerves, the kind that breed missed cues, line stepping, and cotton mouth.

And Television "All the major TV shows." If that was an overstatement, it was only barely so. But a word, first, about the medium. It is an irony of media gestation that television was never so vital or fertile as in its infancy. Before advertisers exploited it as a monstrous electronic billboard and before videotape made slick that which was immediate and raw, network television was not, as it was to become, a convalescent home for fading demicelebrities, but a proving ground for new talent. It has been said that when historians chronicle post-war show business, vaudeville will be spelled "t-e-l-e-v-i-s-i-o-n." Here was a unique median between stage and screen, at once live and optical, and brimming with opportunity. Here was an incubator where John Uhler Lemmon III could hatch into Jack Lemmon.

The first television exposure came on the *Kraft Theater* where Jack won a part in "The Arrival of Kitty," based on the venerable warhorse, *Charley's Aunt*. From there, it was a short step to CBS and Worthington Miner's production of the Paul Vincent Carroll play, *Shadow and Substance*. And then it

With Margaret O'Brien, Herbert Marshall, and Gladys Cooper in "The Mystery of 13" on Playhouse 90, October 24, 1957

On Person to Person with Charles Collingwood, October 8, 1959

was off to the races. Jack shuttled between networks for appearances on *Studio One*, *Robert Montgomery Presents*, and even *I Remember Mama*. Working with such budding directorial talent as John Frankenheimer, Sidney Lumet, and Arthur Penn, and such ascending actors as Rod Steiger and Charlton Heston, Jack was keeping very good company.

Lightning finally struck when Jack was approached by Charles Irving at ABC to take the featured role in an interim series, *That Wonderful Guy*, formerly *The Kid from Kalamazoo*. It struck twice when Cynthia Stone was awarded the female lead over another blonde ingenue, Eva Marie Saint. Short-lived at only seventeen weeks, the series still helped open new doors, increasingly with dual offers for this affable "husband and wife" team. It was only a matter of time before life imitated art, and the two became a certified pair on May 7, 1950 in Cynthia's home town of

Peoria, Illinois. A brief Miami honeymoon, and they were back in the television maelstrom, first with a CBS filler called *The Ad-libbers* and then with a regular featured spot as *The Couple Next Door* on ABC's daily hour-long show with Don Ameche and Frances Langford.

Aware that the Lemmon twosome had become eminently marketable, CBS lured them back with a show called *Jack Loves Cinnie*, charitably changed to *Heaven for Betsy*. The series was aimed at denting the immense popularity of a certain vehicle for recycled talents known as *I Love Lucy*, but the Lemmons were simply not up to the antic inanity of formula comedy. *Heaven for Betsy* took a hard look at the competition, then rolled over and played dead.

But like the Old Knick, death in television was only as permanent as the next show. With and without Cynthia, Jack bounced from performance to performance, and in a five-year tenure, amassed, by his count, some 500 credits—give or take a hundred. By any count, it made for a prodigious resumé.

Then, in a word, the questionnaire got to the matter at hand. *Play* "Room Service," that is, a revival of the sensational 1937 farce with Sam Levene and Eddie Albert, which was devastated on film the following year by the Marx Brothers. *Role* "Leo Davis—playwright from Oswego" and one of the premier rube roles of popular theater. *Producer* "Hart," Bernard, brother to Moss. *Theatre* "Playhouse", at 48th Street, a ten-minute walk from Grand Central Station. Back in 1946, Jack had figured it was merely a five-hour train ride from Boston to Broadway. His train was late, by about seven years.

And finally, rounding out the particulars, the questionnaire asked: *Hair* "black," *Eyes* "hazel," *Height* "6'11"." 6'11"? That's how tall Jack Lemmon felt, that mid-December morning.

Young Lemmon

Many actors begin in film as leading men. Many more end that way. It is another of Hollywood's semantic somersaults that "the leading man" seldom leads anything and rarely is manly. Worse yet, an actor is never so much "a" leading man as "her" leading man, throwing the entire term into the possessive and out of the expressive. It's a little like being a dramatic gigolo, living on borrowed fame, relying on ill-gotten patronage. These were the sobering facts of life Jack Lemmon was due to face.

Room Service opened in early April and ran all the way to the end of the month. The producer passed it off as a short run, which is a rather flip way of admitting a flop. Either way, it took only eighteen performances to drive home the fact that the anaesthetic fifties were a world apart from the cynical desperation of the thirties. Somehow, starvation, bankruptcy, and blithering Russian waiters were no longer as rollicking as they had been twenty years earlier. Not even the creditable presence of Everett Sloane and Alexander Asro (who originated the role of Sasha Smirnoff, the waiter) could rescue the play from the erosion of time.

For Jack Lemmon, this was to be a very successful failure. As the befuddled Leo Davis, he had brought new life to the dormant tradition of the comic victim, and

PULVER-IZED

"You'll find I'm honest, thrifty and methodical, sober, upright, and really kind of dull."—as Robert Tracy in *Phffft!*, 1954

had done so under the scrutiny of a motion picture talent scout. The air was soon thick with contract negotiations, and, while later accounts were quick to categorize this as one more example of the sanctified stage-screen alliance, the truth is that television had been the prime mover.

Weeks before *Room Service* even opened, Max Arnow, head of talent for Columbia Pictures, was unwinding in front of the television set, conducting his subliminal nightly talent hunt. The fare happened to be *Robert Montgomery Presents* which that evening featured Diana Lynn and an actor named Lemmon. "I was taken with this fellow, with the strong personality. In those days, most of the stars were the typical handsome young man rather than the sort who could get by on character and personality. Jack was handsome but not the typical romantic image."

Arnow obtained a kinescope copy of the program and sent it to studio head Harry Cohn, who then relayed it to director George Cukor. Cukor was shopping for a leading man to play opposite Judy Holliday, and she being a decidedly

PHFFFT! (1954). As Robert Tracy

unique star, he was eager to provide a companionable personality. On the strength of the one television appearance, Lemmon had generated enough interest to warrant the dispatching of a studio scout to New York and the 48th Street Playhouse.

The chance jumped at Jack, not the reverse. After five years in television, he was no careerist looking to lunge at the first film contract dangled in his direction.* Television had furnished an invaluable paid apprenticeship, and had opened its doors when the theater world had come to look like a sealed vault. Lemmon, now a journeyman, was not about to jump leagues, even experimentally, without a good reason. The standard screen test with a forty-week option wasn't reason enough. Jack suggested a few of his own: a seven-year, non-exclusive contract with a minimum of two pictures per year and an option for a third; plus, an allowance for scattered television work and as many as four plays, for the duration of the contract terms. Here was no patsy.

Reasonably sure he had bartered himself out of an offer, Jack kept busy while his bill of rights filtered back to the Columbia high command. The response was alarmingly swift—"agreed", conditional on a positive screen test. As Lemmon packed his bags, he fancied himself "Jack, the giant killer," but only fleetingly. His mind was preoccupied with other thoughts, mostly with the fact that he was going alone.

There are any number of theories on why marriage between professionals is prone to collapse. And yet, on the face of it, the relationship between Jack and Cynthia was ideal. Both were working, both advancing. Money had ceased to be a worry, and they had, in fact, moved into a cheerful, spacious apartment on stylish Sutton Place. With their wire-haired terrier, Duffy, they might have been a latter-day Nick and Nora Charles, right down to their Asta. Their problems were clearly not generic, they were human. "We were best friends," Cynthia explains. "We did love each other, but it was all a performance. We had great fun together, and I'm sure to onlookers we were 'The Couple Next Door.' But we did not have a successful marriage." Jack's work in *Room Service* only widened the gulf between them, since he had taken the part in addition to television duties, not instead of them. Had there been the inclination to resolve differences, there still wasn't the time. In early 1953, Jack and Cynthia began a trial separation.

When John Barrymore first set foot in Hollywood, he was ac-

---

*Lemmon had an earlier brush with film as a bit player in a short subject, *You Bet Your Life*.

IT SHOULD HAPPEN TO YOU (1954). With Judy Holliday

corded a hero's welcome. Jack Lemmon slipped into town and made straight for the Hollywood Roosevelt Hotel. He reported to the studio the next morning and with little preparation and even less ceremony, he executed a screen test for the Holliday film, then tentatively called *A Name for Herself*. The test started shakily but finished smoothly, and while it was being processed and prepared for screening, Jack was invited to test for another Columbia film, *The Long Gray Line*, which director John Ford was then casting.

The tests groped their way through the studio hierarchy, and on May 15th, sentence was pronounced: *The Long Gray Line* was out of the question; *A Name for Herself* was Lemmon's for the asking. He was asking. Jack became Judy's leading man and right away bulk became a problem—except for his slight height advantage, they were virtually the same size. Among other things, this was to be Jack's introduction to shoulder padding and shoe lifts.

Size aside, all other signs were auspicious. For one, this was only Holliday's second film since her Oscar-winning starring debut in *Born Yesterday* (1950), and the prospects were still good for a sympathetic hit. With a script by Garson Kanin, who had co-authored Holliday's last film, *The Marrying Kind*, and a directorial encore by George Cukor, the odds improved mightily. So solid were the key credentials that the novice Lemmon might have felt like a fifth wheel, had he not been welcomed into the fold with a warmth and regard generally reserved for more tested talents. This ready cordiality went far to ease a tenseness which surfaced in his acting as self-consciousness. It became evident that Jack's technique owed more to stage than screen, but then, Cukor, Kanin, and Holliday had all been theatre bred. That awareness, plus Cukor's gentle prompting of "Less, less, my boy", introduced Jack to the energetic but intimate acting style that was to become the signature of his early film work. His instincts were so quick to adjust to the new medium that he was soon suggesting touches and bits of business which the seasoned director gladly adopted. *A Name for Herself* completed its studio segments, swept off to New York for some additional location footage, and returned to Hollywood in early summer, just in time to find it had been renamed *It Should Happen to You*, placing it in the vanguard of fifties' overworded titles.

It Should Happen to You (1954)

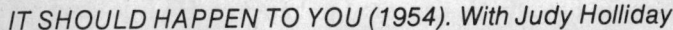

IT SHOULD HAPPEN TO YOU (1954). With Judy Holliday

is probably best remembered as an inoffensive and forgettable film. It is a fanciful but familiar installment in Hollywood's inexhaustible "what price success" genre. The candidate here is Gladys Glover, a doe-eyed dunce from upstate New York, who comes to the city to make her fortune. Girdle modeling is as close as she gets, and she loses even that after exceeding the prescribed maximum bulge by three quarters of an inch. She despairs of the whole business, and, in retreat, bumps into a free-lance documentary maker, Pete Sheppard (Lemmon) at Central Park's Bethesda Fountain. They exchange woes, and she gets the notion that the answer to her appetite for fame is self-advertisement, literally. Using the last of her savings, Gladys rents a Columbus Circle billboard and posts her name and picture, in what amounts to the largest photo resumé in history. The exposure catapults her into the public eye and, that done, she becomes a salable commodity by simple virtue of her celebrity. Her talent is her visibility; she is well known for being well-known.

Gladys wins fame, loses Pete's respect, and attracts the amorous advances of wealthy playboy and soap scion, Evan Adams III (Peter Lawford). Inevitably, the champion of self-promotion realizes that there's more to life than wealth, glamour, and penthouses—there's moderation, conformity, and rooming houses. In an updated rendition of thirties' Horatio Alger gone sour, Gladys goes from girdles to riches and back again. She runs off with Pete, proving once again that the truest fulfillment is to be found at life's lower rungs.

As the sensible and sardonic Sheppard, the ivied Lemmon may not have been central casting's idea of a salt-of-the-earth filmmaker, even by scrubbed fifties' norms. But that's where the second guessing stops. Where another, less versatile actor might have chosen a single aspect of the role and played it safely to the hilt, Lemmon explores the implied dimensions and welds them into a credible unit, a character. He is leading man, comic foil, comedian, and character actor, all blended in a naturalistic delivery of gum-chewing, head-bobbing, brow-knitting, and word-groping that leaves an impression of spontaneity rare among supporting roles. One look at Peter Lawford's smarmy, slickered playboy, which is admittedly fine caricature work, is all that's necessary for an appreciation of the fullness of Lemmon's character work. Their respective Holliday scenes accent that distinction.

On screen with Lawford, Holliday resorts to the dimpled dithering that marked her Billie Dawn in *Born Yesterday*. Together, they enact the cliché-filled script at a

IT SHOULD HAPPEN TO YOU (1954). With Judy Holliday

PHFFFT! (1954). With Judy Holliday

literal level, which bares the many flaws and throws an unflattering light on Holliday's basic comic makeup—that she is a large lady with a little voice.

Lemmon, on the other hand, humanizes her through his own sensitivity. She is as good as her company, and he is the best. They wring the dialogue of every worthy syllable, and where the script falters, they find undercurrents of warmth and wiliness that would easily have escaped most performers. Their teamwork is shown to best advantage in a cozy bar scene where Lemmon and Holliday share a few bars of "Let's Fall in Love" with Jack comfortably at the keyboard. The freshness, timing, and frankness is all there in what can only be described as rapport.

Apart from Judy, Jack is still assured, but in so subtle a fashion that he often insinuates himself into a scene rather than entering coldly. He seems to emerge from the very background, and to dissolve there again at will. This ability to throw his presence in and out of focus is an expert way of rationing his personality, which, with its assortment of tics and pool of energy, is wisely harnessed. While his body

PHFFFT! (1954). With Kim Novak

seems coiled but collected, his facial features are active and his dialogue virtually acrobatic. Lemmon variously winnows and wallops his words, enunciating and mumbling, stammering with metrical precision. His banter with Holliday is clipped, and it punctuates the glissando of her helium voice. In a particularly heated argument stoked by an exaggerated note of finality, Lemmon exits as if forever, waits a classic three beats, and then stomps back to ask "So is it still on for Saturday night?"—a line he himself conceived. Like the finest comic actors, he is able to use his own folly as foil.

It Should Happen to You no sooner finished shooting than there were murmurs about a prodigy on the lot. Jack read the portents and decided that whatever was to happen to his career, would have to happen in Hollywood. It was a time for fresh starts, and marriage topped the list. Cynthia joined Jack on the coast, and they promptly purchased a home in Brentwood on Kenter Avenue off Sunset Boulevard.

This pre-release period was also a time for studio acclimation. Jack was ordered to Harry Cohn's office and there faced the ritual sparring for which the gruff studio boss was famed and feared. The name had to go. "Nobody can be in films with that name. The critics will use it like a baseball bat. They'll crucify you." Lemmon was to become Lennon, but there was a minor hitch—Jack flatly refused. Except for a faint-hearted moment in *Power of Darkness*, he had come this far sounding of citrus, and saw no reason to change. Cohn jabbed away, but Lemmon returned blow for blow and emerged triumphant, which as insiders knew, was the fastest way to the bully's heart. Lemmon not only remained Lemmon, he became Harry's Harvard Man.

It Should Happen to You opened in January of 1954 and was a hit. Reviews were especially abuzz over this new comic actor. Jack became an official hot property and as such was not to be spent on just any script. He may have been a "find" but he didn't feel particularly found; he was forced to wait a full seven months for the proper vehicle to roll up to Columbia's front door.

In a stroke typical of Hollywood imagination and daring, Jack was at last returned to the screen—opposite Judy Holliday. After lying fallow for so long, a fertile phase seemed in the offing, and subsequent news of Cynthia's pregnancy was taken as a token of things to come. The baby arrived in June of 1954 and was called Christopher. The film arrived in November of that year and was called *Phffft!* Christopher was a bouncing, healthy 9½ pounds. *Phffft!* was a

THREE FOR THE SHOW (1955). With Betty Grable and Gower Champion

limp, lame ninety minutes and, according to critics, was a motion picture stillborn.

Lemmon plays a withdrawn tax lawyer husband to Holliday's yammering author wife. As if to remind us how well they squabbled in their previous collaboration, the film begins with the end of their marriage, providing an excuse for a sultry, overfed Kim Novak to explain that "phffft" is the sound of a marriage in ruin.

The two go their separate ways. He continues to rifle receipts and she supervises her daytime serial, *Serena Noble, Doctor's Wife*. But through a design that the film would pass off as chance, their paths cross frequently enough to touch off a competition wherein each attempts to out-cavort the other. Enter Jack Carson, the heel's heel, and Kim Novak, the vamp-in-training, respectively lusting after the newly unweds. The naughtiness goes for naught as they all only manage to out-embarrass one another. The film milks its situation dry, then wraps the remains in a trite ribbon of reconciliation.

True to its cartoon title, *Phffft!* is

little more than a series of obvious sketches leading to an obligatory conclusion. George Axelrod's script is to blame with its habit of supplying scenes with spoken captions instead of dialogue. It is a format approach, methodical, unimaginative, and tricked up with stale in-joking and leering double-entendre. The script's least forgivable crime is the rank frittering of Lemmon and Holliday. As before, they flatter one another visually and comedically, cuddling and feuding with comparable charm. The two make a wonderfully adult couple, but the dialogue is woefully adolescent. One can only imagine how they might have soared with a bright Ben Hecht or Billy Wilder screenplay as a springboard.

For a comic actor, a bad script is a crucial test, the more so for one of Lemmon's dynamic style. Many will strain for effect, squeezing a bad line for life or broadening takes for notice. In *Phffft!*, Lemmon is a model of restraint, aside from where the script absolutely demands otherwise. His underplaying softens the film's banality and accelerates its tempo, hinting of that all-important comic credo—if you're dying, do it quick-

THREE FOR THE SHOW (1955). With Betty Grable and Gower Champion

ly. Other funereal lessons were in store for Lemmon.

There are dancers who sing a little, singers who dance a little, and actors who do neither. There is a little of each in Lemmon's next film, *Three for the Show* (1955), a musical based on a play by W. Somerset Maugham that had been filmed in 1940 as *Too Many Husbands*. Designed as a Technicolor tonic for Betty Grable, the cast includes Marge and Gower Champion, with Lemmon slipping to a lowly fourth billing.

Typically, the musical hinges on the slimmest of plots. Lemmon, a former playwright now pilot, is believed killed on an aerial mission in Korea. His actress wife, Grable, enters into a ricochet romance with her late husband's best friend, a dancer played by Gower Champion, a dancer. Still another dancer, Marge Champion, has had eyes for both men but no luck with either. According to form, following the wedding between the widowed wife and the best friend, Lemmon shows up in the flesh and, appraised of the situation, angrily points out that his wife is no longer widowed nor, for that matter, is his friend best any more. But this is a musical, and nothing like simplicity is allowed before the final reel. A paragon of fairness, Grable sizes up the predicament, "If I decide on one of you, I've got to hurt the other, and I love you both too much for that." She is willing to hold auditions for the spot, however, which becomes the coy premise until Lemmon tires of the triangular life, and takes a powder. There are some last minute "show must go on" heroics which return Lemmon to Grable's embrace, and, naturally, reveal that the Champions were always meant for each other.

The plot, which is really a half-dozen plots and therefore no plot at all, serves as a wide net for several lush, candy-colored production numbers. Betty Grable, leggy, shapely, and peppy as ever, never looked lovelier; and her thirty-nine-year-old midriff, bared for a Latin dance, is as firm and tapered as a young chorine's. The Champions confirm their undiminished gift for musical comedy, and contribute some spiffy and spoofing dance duets. And, though his input dwindles in the most elaborately staged scenes, Lemmon is never dead weight. He sustains the comic moments, improves what little narrative continuity there is, and even elevates the lacquered Gower Champion to new heights of repartée. Looking tanned and fit, Lemmon complements Grable's platinum gloss, and if a bit to the tender side of her age, he is not so green as to make her seem overripe. Even though Lemmon shrinks within the full-blown numbers, he shines in a modest offering of the Gershwins' "I've Got a Crush on

MISTER ROBERTS (1955). *As Ensign Pulver*

You", accompanying Grable as she sings, and even crooning a verse of his own.

Lemmon employs a sly musical-comedy survival strategy. Without towering talents of voice or step, he transforms himself into a character actor. His style is abbreviated into mannerism, preventing him from appearing mannered alongside the tissue-thin story. The veteran character actor, Myron McCormick, is on hand and serves as a convenient scale for Jack's approach. Lemmon measures up, even for all the frill and fun of *Three for the Show*.

When Jack tested for *The Long Gray Line*, all he had heard was "no." What he hadn't heard was John Ford's reaction to a specific makeup segment, "That kid makes the worst old man I ever saw. But he'd be a hell of a Pulver." He was referring to his upcoming filming of *Mister Roberts* (1955) for Warner Brothers. Lemmon knew nothing in particular of the film or the director; he didn't even know what Ford looked like. So it wasn't surprising that when Jack decided to drop by the set of *The Long Gray Line* to see how Tyrone Power was weathering the lead, he thought nothing of shooting the breeze with a certain tattered gaffer wearing an eye patch and chewing absently on the corner of a handkerchief. As legend has it, the conversation went like this: "You Lemmon?" "Yeah." "I've been watching you. You know something, they're going to make *Mister Roberts* soon and you'd make a good Pulver." "Spread the word." "You want to play the part?" "In the world, there is no part I want to play more." "Okay, spit in your hand." "Huh?" "Spit in your hand, it's an old Irish custom. There, I'm Ford and you're Pulver." A firmer pact was never made.

Some months later, work began on location in Hawaii and on Midway Island. Starting with the play, which had opened on Broadway in 1948 and was an instant success, the production seemed gilded. The Thomas Heggen-Joshua Logan yarn, about life aboard a backwater cargo ship in the Pacific during World War II, brimmed with choice roles. Casting was an invitation for coup. Of the many actors who braced the Broadway run, only Henry Fonda was asked to repeat—an inevitability since he had virtually metabolized the title role of Lieutenant Roberts. James Cagney was drafted as the ship's captain and William Powell its doctor. Add the direction of crusty John Ford, himself a Navy veteran, and the cinematography of Winton Hoch, an Oscar winner for *She Wore a Yellow Ribbon* (1949), and the entire project seemed failsafe.

Shooting began on schedule and continued apace. In step with the regimental Ford, the cast lived a

MISTER ROBERTS (1955). With William Powell

fraternal barracks life of burly companionship, good-natured pranking, and sporadic scuffles. Lemmon quickly found his spot in the pecking order, and just as quickly forged a friendship with Cagney, who remembered Jack from television. The two passed the time with the former vaudeville hoofer tutoring the young tanglefoot in a few turns. On the set, though, all was business.

As Pulver, Lemmon was to be, among other things, impish and impulsive. As director, Ford liked to menace actors into their roles, and he adopted a ploy of keeping Lemmon off balance with juggled set calls and unscheduled shooting. Jack was already too professional to be unnerved by the tactics, just as he was already too naturally nervous not to be frenetic as Pulver. He gave the director no call to regret that moist handshake some months earlier.

By the time the company returned from location for studio footage, the young actor had learned a great deal. "The people who worked with Ford had a love-hate relationship with him. I suppose he could be a tyrant at times, but he was a great director, a giant." He was also mortal, and the production no sooner returned to Hollywood than Ford was rushed to the hospital for emergency gall bladder surgery. The optimistic mood changed overnight, even after the reputable Mervyn LeRoy was announced as replacement. LeRoy moved to assuage any doubts, and called a cast meeting where he detailed his intention to finish shooting in Ford's style. Given the fact that primarily interiors remained, the claim was plausible, and commendable.

Mister Roberts went to the cutting room, and Jack prepared to settle down to a home life that had again grown unsettled. But back at Warners, the first screenings produced some uneasy tremors. The film was faithful to the play, perhaps too faithful. There was no theatricality, but the pace was heavily proscenium with little filmic reduction. It was not the sort of slowness that could be corrected by deletion, so the opposite was attempted. Lemmon, who accounted for most of what velocity was present, was summoned to the lab and told to limber up his vocal chords. The idea was to post-synchronize some harmless, a cappella tune over the long and medium Pulver shots. Jack selected a thirties ditty, "If I Could Be With You", and muttered, hummed, and warbled a handful of renditions which were then superimposed on the sound track. As it worked out, the melody not only picked up the pace by several beats, but helped peg Lemmon as the film's surprise favorite.

All things considered, *Mister Roberts* still wobbles. The story of an officer's struggle to enter active combat duty is without a convincing time frame. The war is in scant evidence, and so Roberts's enthusiasm seems misplaced, more as if he were hankering for a World Series or a circus that comes to town but once. Since his frustrations are the film's central conflict, all else is thrown out of context. Fonda's handling of Roberts does nothing to remedy matters. His careful voice modulations become monotone. His moods lack range and become merely moody. His performance, like his presence, is lanky. Cagney, meanwhile, is underdirected. It is never completely clear whether his captain is truly some sadistic petty despot or just a buffoon with chronic heartburn. As the ship's doctor, Powell is better used, though his urbane grace is lost on the setting.

Leads aside, a still greater obstacle is the supporting cast. The nurses, added for the screenplay, are window dressing and not to be faulted, but the ship's crew is flat and flavorless. Granted, the Navy was something of a military elite, yet the film would have benefited from less authenticity and more ethnicity—no kettle bubbles so appealingly as a melting pot; certainly that much was established in Billy

Wilder's estimable *Stalag 17* (1953). The crew of the cargo vessel *S. S. Reluctant* might just as well be the Harvard Glee Club, and the film suffers for the blondness and blandness.

With some one hundred years of motion picture experience represented in key spots of the production, it is the rookie to the rescue. Jack Lemmon, all of four films old, keeps *Mister Roberts* afloat. His Pulver is sheer inspiration, distinct from David Wayne's stage interpretation of the role. A would-be satyr, he is really more a horse's ass, in Roberts's estimate "the most hapless, lazy, disorganized, and in general the most lecherous person I've ever known in my life." Who could resist such a total slob?

Lemmon's portrayal is anything but sloppy. Pulver becomes a ready reservoir of the actor's energy, kinetic and precise, immediately knowable but not predictable—a masterpiece of character acting. Most importantly, Lemmon does not clown the role. He executes it at a sincere, naive level, drawing himself up neatly into Pulver's absurdity. Beyond the chipper gait, which might have rubbed off in the dance lessons with Cagney, it is all Lemmon.

If work well done is its own reward, a little added recognition is a welcome bonus. Lemmon collected his bonus at that year's Academy Awards ceremony, in the category of best supporting actor. It was the end of his motion picture initiation and the beginning of his problems.

MISTER ROBERTS (1955). With Henry Fonda

Next to the jump cut and the dissolve, the character actor is the closest movies have come to cinematic shorthand. A good character actor can cue a time, a place, a mood, or even an emotion. But his worth is also his doom. Studios are slow to hazard a known quantity on anything so elusive as stardom. Character actors tend to remain character actors.

In most cases, a best supporting Oscar is a little like having "character actor" tattooed across the forehead. Pulver might have been poison to Jack's long-term ambitions, but that was a secondary worry at the time. His marriage had taken a sudden, sharp downturn and within weeks of the awards ceremony, he and Cynthia were quietly filing for divorce. "The Couple Next Door" chalked it up to incompatability, and politely carved up the property. As Jack remembers, "There was never any unpleasantness. If you can have such a thing, I guess you could say we had a very successful divorce." Successful was more than could be said of the material Columbia was handing him.

Reluctant to commit Lemmon to a single image, the studio delivered him to that actor's purgatory known as the musical—a pair of purgatories, in fact, neither of which was original. The first, *My Sister Eileen* (1955), had been refurbished more times than an old

JACK'S DILEMMA

"If I told you once, I told you a thousand times. It never pays to get mixed up with human beings."—as Nicky Holroyd in *Bell, Book and Candle*, 1958

gaberdine. Based on a series of short stories by Ruth McKenney, it first reached the stage in 1940 with some handy midwifery from Jerome Chodorov and Joseph Fields. *Eileen* found its way to film in 1942 with Rosalind Russell, and then scampered back to the stage as a musical, *Wonderful Town*, with words and music by Betty Comden, Adolph Green, and Leonard Bernstein. When *Eileen* resurfaced in 1955, it was basically its 1940 self, but wearing new songs by Jule Styne and Leo Robin. The history may be more interesting than the movie.

This fourth serving stars Janet Leigh as the dreamy dish, Eileen, and Betty Garrett as her sardonic sister, Ruth. Actress and writer, respectively, they come to New York from Ohio in search of fame and fortune. They find a grimy Greenwich Village basement apartment, a shifty landlord, and more closed doors than they had dreamed were possible. On balance, they do win suitors aplenty, even the not-so-ugly-duckling Ruth. It takes just over an hour and a half for the film to sort out the romance. By that time, Eileen is taken with a bemused soda jerk, Frank Lippencott, and Ruth succumbs to an eccentric magazine publisher, Bob Baker.

A dancer by trade, Bob Fosse makes his singing debut as the starry-eyed Lippencott. No Mario Lanza, he still has a way with a tune and more than compensates with his vigorous dance numbers. An actor by trade, Jack Lemmon's publisher does not enter until the third reel, and even then hovers mostly at the edges of the action. He gets the most out of his few lines, and comes to the fore in a teasing cat-and-canary scene with Betty Garrett, which he caps with a bouncy song of seduction, "It's Bigger than You and Me."

Soon, one song begins to sound like the next, but the refreshing dancing of Leigh, Garrett, and Fosse staves off musical amnesia. Director Richard Quine (who played Lippencott on Broadway in 1940) keeps his wits about him and propels the film with an eye to fun—after all, *My Sister Eileen* is a musical. *You Can't Run Away From It* (1956), another remake, is a catastrophe.

Lemmon had learned a lasting

At the Academy Award ceremonies in 1956: presenter Edmond O'Brien with winner Jo Van Fleet (East of Eden), and presenter Eva Marie Saint with winner Jack Lemmon (Mister Roberts)

MY SISTER EILEEN (1955). With Betty Garrett and Janet Leigh

mathematical lesson in *Room Service*: The thirties, plus twenty years, does not equal the fifties; it equals anachronism. Dick Powell, who serenaded his way through a number of indelible Depression musicals, should have known of the equation. But he was just getting his feet wet as a director and had much to learn, such as, don't tinker with classic motion pictures; don't cast your wife unless you are Vincente Minnelli; and never remake a screwball comedy as a musical. Powell broke each rule, and by any count it was three strikes against him. The real casualty was his picture, *You Can't Run Away From It* (1956), a musical rehash of *It Happened One Night* (1934).

Frank Capra's original was a landmark motion picture. It signalled the coming of that sophisticated slapstick, screwball comedy, and at the same time opened a subgenre of so-called "runaway heiress" stories. It was the first film to sweep all the major Academy Awards, and it had the audacity to reveal that Clark Gable did not wear an undershirt. Most other comedies pale by comparison. Powell's film all but shrivels and blows away.

June Allyson, then married to Powell, takes the role that had been

Claudette Colbert's, the bratty, impetuous Ellie Andrews—not a little like recasting a silk purse as a sow's ear. Allyson's slight personality is incapable of the elegant wit and elite naiveté required here. Her schoolyard charm merely emphasizes the disparity and hints of a telltale dowdiness. Frankly, she seems less a madcap heiress and more a maiden aunt.

In Gable's role of the smug-lug reporter, Peter Warne, Lemmon is like a kid in the attic. The character sags on him like Dad's old suit. Lemmon, the hyperactive collegiate, has no feel for the hard-luck, hard-boiled denizen of the working press he portrays, nor has he Gable's beefy masculine appeal. Witness Jack's barechested bedroom scene, which scarcely stirs a tremble where his predecessor's version practically registered on the Richter scale. Were he even able to crank up his machismo, it still would have been misspent on Allyson. Her rag doll image is sexually prohibitive, and she and Lemmon collide with all the spark of two sponges.

As if this were not matter enough, the film is marred by a host of technical faux pas in lighting, editing, and even fundamental continuity. The camera work never opens up, and is detectably dawdling on Allyson. The music offers no lift, and the supporting actors represent the final nails in the coffin. None of this escaped Jack's attention. Reading a few choice words over the grave of *You Can't Run Away From It*, he bid a less than fond farewell to the Powells.

With his marriage a shambles and his career slumping, Jack was primed for a change. Word of an action thriller, planned for location shooting in Trinidad and England, was all the bait he needed. Had he examined the script more closely, he would have been less hasty.

Fire Down Below (1957) bills Rita Hayworth and Robert Mitchum above Lemmon in a film that begins as a tacky and trite adventure romance, and ends with a squirmingly dramatic passage that is as unexpected as a tense high-wire act in a shabby sideshow. Mitchum and Lemmon play a pair of small-time smugglers who come to blows over an entrancing cargo, Hayworth. It is a tenuous tandem to begin with: Mitchum as a sleazy sailor and Lemmon as his gawky sidekick, a bit like teaming Captain Hook and Peter Pan. Hayworth is, as ever, the woman with a past, although it's not entirely clear whether this is the same past she has had in other films, or some new past. In any case, the kid falls for her like bricks and his briny partner takes pains to demonstrate that such women deserve only abuse and animal lust. There is a brawl followed by treachery, and Lemmon is

MY SISTER EILEEN (1955). With Kurt Kasznar

nearly killed in a last solo smuggling mission meant to finance a future with Hayworth, so that she can forget that past which no one can seem to remember anyway.

The real dramatics are ushered in when Lemmon signs on with a Greek freighter and is trapped below in a foggy midnight collision. The forward hold of raw rubber catches fire and smolders aft where there are eighty tons of nitrate, leaving Lemmon in the middle of a titanic time bomb. Drastic measures are considered after attempts to free him fail. There is talk of amputation and, that refused, mention of suicide. Death seems imminent when a penultimate minor blast frees the trapped Lemmon who then scrambles to safety moments before the freighter makes like an oversized firecracker. That still leaves a score to settle with Mitchum, but plot is thicker than water, and the two emerge friends—an anticlimax that rates as the film's biggest smuggle of all.

Fire Down Below is best appreciated as two films in one. The first is a bawdy, gaudy piece of pulp with the then popular "limbo" music blaring out of every cranny. Rather than act, Mitchum simply parcels his off-screen image as a boozy womanizer. Hayworth, who is voluptuous as ever, even if her décolletage has to sneak lower to capture the effect, does what she does best, presenting a charismatic tramp with a conscience. In her defense, it should be noted that she is fettered with some of the worst dialogue of a painfully bad lot, at turns puzzling over sexual politics, "Sometimes you wonder what God had in mind when he invented the male sex," or recalling her wicked past, "I've lived among the ruins. Armies have marched over me. I've been debased." The confettied Technicolor pays her no compliment, and the direction is disastrously piecemeal, to the disadvantage of all.

Then there is the drama in the ship's hold, which of its own is really movie enough. Where Lemmon begins as foolish and callow, he takes on a gritty, cynical aspect. His strength is his quiet desperation, asserting his personal bitterness over the false optimism of his erstwhile rescuers. Unfortunately, Lemmon's incisive dramatic work is undercut by the implausible last-minute escape from doom, and the textual emptiness of the impending showdown with Mitchum all but erases the preceding segment. Blame Irwin Shaw's screenplay and Robert Parrish's direction. The film's innocuous harmonica score is Lemmon's, for better or worse.

The travel, if not the film, did Jack good and he returned to Hollywood revitalized. The mood was contagious, and Columbia was ready to see if their proven supporting actor could carry an entire film. Lemmon's good friend, Richard Quine, was chosen to direct, and the designated property was a modest service comedy from a play by Arthur Carter. The happy result is *Operation Mad Ball* (1957), a sturdy, playful outing in black and white that flies in the face of such consecrated material as *Mister Roberts*.

Prior to shooting, Quine had set himself up as a Lemmon-watcher: "It's tough to make him believable in a love scene. You put him with a femme fatale and for some reason she will seem to overpower him; maybe because of the boyish quality he has." Lemmon's sober reply, "Quine is full of crap. As screen lovers go, I'm a biggie." The issue remained temporarily unresolved, since *Operation Mad Ball* was by no means a likely crucible for romance.

Unpretentious as it is, the film is a standout among Lemmon's early screen work. It tells the tangled tale of a frisky collection of enlisted men in post-war Normandy, scheming to throw an unsanctioned party under the inquisitive nose of an ironclad captain. It is a glorified prank that sets up its

YOU CAN'T RUN AWAY FROM IT (1956).
With June Allyson

YOU CAN'T RUN AWAY FROM IT (1956).
With June Allyson

situations with accuracy, and knocks them off one after another with cheerful speed. Private Al Hogan, the highly decorated and unscrupulously resourceful ringleader, calculates the logistics with the precision of a miniature D-Day. Despite some elaborate counter-scheming by the captain, and a romantic mix-up or two, the romp comes to pass as the promised "mad ball."

The jumbled shenanigans notwithstanding, *Operation Mad Ball* is a tightly tailored article of film work. Quine's camera never lags, but moves the story along with just the right blend of slapstick, gaiety, and romantic intrigue. Yet, the film comes together best at the character level. Here, Lemmon as Hogan is the comic hub, a canny epicenter that sets things in motion without appearing to spin in place. Back in uniform, Lemmon performs in a facile, aggressive spirit. His timing is magnificent both as perpetrator and victim, and his physique has assumed a manly fullness of face and figure, which budges his scenes with Kathryn Grant beyond the usual note of obligatory amour, Quine's claims to the contrary.

Lemmon's manic drive is at full tilt, and it actively enlivens the rather ordinary supporting cast. Commonly colorless personalities like Dick York, Roger Smith, and James Darren suddenly spring to life. Old hand Arthur O'Connell

FIRE DOWN BELOW (1957). With Rita Hayworth

FIRE DOWN BELOW (1957). With Robert Mitchum

OPERATION MAD BALL (1957). With Dick York and Mickey Rooney

offers leavening, while the adrenalized Mickey Rooney supplies a wildly scatty character that pulls up just short of exhaustion. In a first foray from television, Ernie Kovacs volunteers a splendid slice of arch villainy as the spoilsport captain. From top to bottom, *Operation Mad Ball* is well-packed ensemble work in the best sense of slickness.

On the crest of favorable critical response, Lemmon then became officially "versatile." But there were limits to experimentation. He chose to draw the line at Westerns, not for self-doubt but because of a nagging aversion to horses that dated back to his youth and a succession of Sunday morning rides atop a sadistic Shetland pony named "Pepper." The grounds for refusal only sharpened the interest of Harry Cohn, who was casting a Frank Harris story about a desk clerk's initiation into the rugged world of the cattle drover. No amount of sugar or vinegar could persuade Lemmon, so Cohn, never above subterfuge, conspired with Glenn Ford, who had already signed for the production. Jack was escorted to a tavern across the street from the studio, and besieged with a barrage of martinis. His resistance proved soluble in alcohol, and with all the consciousness necessary to push a pen, he was pointed at a contract. It was not exactly a deal that would hold up in court, but by the time sobriety returned, Jack had thawed on the whole proposition. He would herein be avenged of Pepper.

Frank Harris's *My Reminiscences as a Cowboy* was shortened to *Cowboy* (1958), and is essentially an inventory of life among the cattle. Lemmon plays an overeager hotel clerk who opportunistically bilks his way into Glenn Ford's cattle barony. Without recourse, the autocratic Ford permits the greenhorn to tramp along on the next long drive from range to railhead. The rest is equal parts Chisolm Trail and Social Darwinism. The extant cowboy code is something better befitting a nest of vipers: kill or be killed; each man for himself; and material gain as the only moral incentive—all of which appalls the citified, civilized clerk. Ford takes special pleasure in hammering home the vagaries of the cattle drive, touching off a brutal feud with Lemmon. As is the habit in these affairs, there is an eventual role reversal as the clerk soon outstrips the trail boss for sheer wretchedness. Just as predictably, they then both moderate, the better for each other's company—

OPERATION MAD BALL (1957). With Ernie Kovacs

COWBOY (1958). As Frank Harris

COWBOY (1958). With Glenn Ford

rawhide with heart.

Cowboy will never qualify as realism. It is too hygienic, pat, and Technicolorful. Nor, on the other hand, can it register as epic or mythic commentary, since director Delmer Daves is merely sorting images and not creating heroic icons. That leaves the film on the middle ground of depiction, which is where the cast becomes troublesome. Ford is primarily Ford, typically brooding and marginally psychopathic, with just a pinch of pathos. Lemmon is identifiable as a clerk, but he is too contemporary and benign ever to seem at home on the range. The final alliance between characters falls far short of authenticity, failing even at the sort of stylized synthesis Howard Hawks had extracted between John Wayne and Montgomery Clift in *Red River*. Lemmon, the machine-age man, is conspicuously out of his element. After *Cowboy*, he resolutely left the Western to those more flexible of repertoire and rump.

That did not mean an end to exploration. A defective wrangler is no less a candidate for warlock, which is what Jack became in John Van Druten's tale of Greenwich Village witchery, *Bell, Book and Candle* (1958). It makes an enchanting film, but it is not Lemmon's film. Jimmy Stewart is starred as a befuddled book pub-

BELL, BOOK AND CANDLE (1958). With Elsa Lanchester and Kim Novak

lisher who falls prey to a sumptuous sorceress, Kim Novak. Billed third, Lemmon is demoted to character status, and the company is diabolically divine. Elsa Lanchester's dizzy charm is in full bloom as Novak's aunt. Hermione Gingold is deliciously grotesque as a rival witch, and Ernie Kovacs is beautifully on pitch as the woozy author and student of the occult, who tries to make sense of the whole conjuring community. Richard Quine's direction is first atmospheric, then ethereal, subtly tipping the play's immersed allegory that bohemian, beat culture is indeed otherworldly.

The gangly, bungling, folksy Stewart makes the perfect patsy for the feline allure of Novak, whose ample figure is packed into a wardrobe of somber black outfits. James Wong Howe's gentle color photography tones the film's varied moods, and bathes Novak's skin in a radiant, liquid light.

As the brash, younger brother warlock, Lemmon is a studied specimen of bongo-thumping, beatnik brevity. In league with Kovacs, the characterization sharpens, but there is ultimately too little material with which to work. Jack had blithely signed for the part at the request of Quine, only to discover

BELL, BOOK AND CANDLE (1958). With Elsa Lanchester, Kim Novak, Ernie Kovacs, and James Stewart

that it required no more than a fraction of his ability: "I never had a 'hook' on it. I was just using technique—fishing." *Bell, Book and Candle* held no magic for warlocks.

Lemmon began to flinch at the notion that "Pulver" had sealed his fate. For a highly motivated, imaginative actor, there is scant satisfaction to be had in character walkthroughs. Columbia had not come up with challenging material, and Jack's generosity around the lot gained him nothing. He was nobody's fool, but then again, he was nobody's protegé. With eternal character acting looming like an infernal destiny, Jack Lemmon needed a mentor, and he needed one soon.

WILD, WILDER, WILDEST

"You don't understand, Osgood. I'm a man."—as Jerry in *Some Like it Hot*, 1959

Many actors have ridden to fame on the fortunes of a single, celebrated motion picture. Few have done so wearing lipstick and lace.

The scene: the ballroom of a rambling, late-twenties beach resort. It is after hours, and the orchestra plays a moody two-step while a lone couple glides across the ornate, parquet dance floor. Osgood is in dinner jacket and black tie. Daphne wears a dark diaphanous gown with intricate beadwork. Without warning, the orchestra breaks into a full-blooded tango. Daphne places a rose between her teeth as Osgood twirls her effortlessly in the dim light of dawn. Fade to black.

The interlude might have been lifted from Fitzgerald, except for a minor detail—Daphne is a man, a bass player named Jerry. Just how he happened to be in this fix is the outlandish story of *Some Like It Hot* (1959).

The film, which has nothing to do with a 1939 Bob Hope programmer of the same name, took its premise from a Weimar Germany feature, *Fanfaren der Liebe* (*Fanfares of Love*), by a writer named Thoeren. It was some twenty-five years before an old acquaintance of Thoeren's decided to remake the property as an outrageous farce of gangsters, molls, and musicians. That is how Billy Wilder came to write and direct *Some Like It Hot*. How Jack Lemmon came to star in it is another story.

Word had gotten around town about a pair of comic roles that would have to be performed under peculiar circumstances. It was as much as could be expected from a writer-director who had previously found humor in a Communist Commissar, a German prisoner of war camp, and a freshly shot Hollywood corpse. In other words, actors were not exactly falling over themselves to get the parts. But then, neither were producers in any mad rush to hire Lemmon. Jack laid hold of a script, read Jerry, contemplated Daphne, and calculated the risks. Friends were predicting that the entire project would end in disgrace, with Jack accused of transvestism. Somehow that seemed less threatening than a career of offbeat, chuckleheaded supporting roles. Wilder got around to offering, and Lemmon wasted no time accepting. Tony Curtis was added as the other "male" lead, and after some tricky financial arrangements, Marilyn Monroe was landed in exchange for a sizable wedge of the profits.

The story opens in gangland Chi-

SOME LIKE IT HOT (1959). With Tony Curtis

cago of 1929, replete with spats, speakeasies, and high caliber violins. A pair of honky-tonk musicians, Joe and Jerry, tenor saxophone and bass fiddle, chance upon a St. Valentine's Day garage-side mob slaying. The two escape the scene, but don't escape notice. They sprint over to a booking office and, anxious to get out of town, they pounce on the first two openings—both with an all-girl novelty band. Joe and Jerry are in no position to quibble over small matters like gender.

When next we see them, they are Josephine and Daphne, from their plumed headgear, to their waistless flapper sack dresses, all the way down to their patent leather pumps. They join the band courteously undetected, and continue with the girls by rail for an engagement in Florida. Cavorting with this bevy of platinum cuties is, for Joe and Jerry, a little bit like being dressed as bon-bons and locked in a candy store. And yet, one reach for the goodies and their charade is blown. Frustration reaches fever pitch in the company of a certain Sugar "Kane" Kovalchick (Monroe), the band's ultra-endowed vocalist, ukelele strummer, and all-around showpiece.

Once in Florida, Joe inaugurates another disguise, posing as a demure, frigid heir, impassively wooing the unwitting Sugar. By way of diversionary tactics, Jerry, as Daphne, is left to vamp an aging playboy so that Joe might avail himself of the old boy's yacht. The actual millionaire's name is Osgood Fielding III (Joe E. Brown), which then explains the saucy, resort-side, wee-hour tango with a bass player. Following a last narrow escape from the clutches of the mob, Joe wins Sugar, and a defrocked Daphne levels with Osgood, whose affections remain strangely unaffected by the news.

Beginning with the film's stunning black-and-white photography by Charles Lang Jr., *Some Like It Hot* is a nostalgia grab-bag. For one, it camps the St. Valentine's Day massacre. Beyond that, it presents the archetypally fedora-ed George Raft as the mobster, Spats Columbo, and even has him chiding another coin-flipping hood, "Where did you pick up that cheap trick?"—a trademark that landed Raft himself in the gangster hall of fame in the seminal *Scarface* (1932). It almost goes without saying that Pat O'Brien stalks on as the flap-tongued, racket-busting Irish cop. Throw in Tony Curtis's counterfeit Cary Grant in his pose as the shy scion (a pardonable anachronism since in 1929 Grant was still an unknown named Archibald Leach), and the movie buff stuff is complete.

That may be the meat of the movie, but the acting is the marrow. For all her delays and tantrums, and protests over the monochromatic mounting, Marilyn Monroe is at the peak of her gifts, such as they are. She is poured into a wardrobe of scoop-backed, deep-necked Orry-Kelly gowns, and very nearly spills out on a number of occasions. But her legendary pneumatic presence is balanced by a convincingly gullible and vulnerable naïveté that makes her a wondrous anomaly. It is as if Pollyanna woke up one morning in Mae West's body.

Wilder's patient though caustic direction keeps Monroe on the edge of the fantastic, but prevents her from stumbling into caricature. The performance was not easily siphoned. There were expensive retakes (fifty-nine on one scene), running skirmishes with the staff and cast, and her obstinate, self-merchandising egotism. The end product is a marvel, but one that led Wilder to declare, "I have discussed this with my doctor and psychiatrist and they tell me I'm too old and too rich to go through this again."

In spite of himself, Tony Curtis is also in top form. New to Monroe and farce alike, he induces a method of performance by opposition. He resists Monroe, and that intensifies her sexuality. His body resists the masquerade, and that underscores the mad frivolity of it. To his credit, Curtis moves at a hustler's tempo, leaving his Grant mimicry short of tedium and his manipulation of Lemmon a mere

SOME LIKE IT HOT (1959). With Tony Curtis

SOME LIKE IT HOT (1959). With Marilyn Monroe

exercise of metabolism.

By way of contrast, Lemmon's approach is guileless and fluent. He plays a trusting Costello to Curtis's glowering Abbott, in one of the classic "chump" performances of modern cinema. Like the great silent clowns, Lemmon has the physical agility to look awkward. His Jerry is a half-step behind life, always sprinting to pull even. But Lemmon shrewdly deposits the character on an invisible treadmill—the harder he strives, the faster he gets nowhere. This stylization of the role might tempt pity in the hands of another actor, but Lemmon wards off gross buffoonery with a tasteful control of body and gesture, and side-steps sentiment with a crabby pessimism.

As Daphne, Lemmon is peerless. He rejects Curtis's arch inhibition in favor of candor. Since the role is constructed with a flagrant built-in parody, he has only to play it straight, which in the abstract, is a gutsy decision for an actor to make. Lemmon delivers himself wholly to Wilder's conception, and together they avoid the concealed pitfalls of vulgarity. Daphne is a mask that Jerry wears with varying degrees of sincerity. Always, it is a means to an end (escape, voyeurism, swindle), but that does not rule out amusement along the way. Each line becomes a lightning triple take. Daphne acts, Jerry reacts, and the actor Lemmon reacts to them both. Note the post-tango huddle where Jerry admits to Joe that he is engaged to Osgood (Joe E. Brown). Daphne is flattered, Jerry is mercenarily absorbed in thoughts of alimony, and Lemmon, tipped by his tone, cringes at the whole affair. It is a crosscurrent style that matches Wilder's own vision, particle for particle. Here, unmistakably, is a rare communion between actor and director.

Tolling a running time of just over two hours (suicidal by comedy standards, let alone farce), *Some Like It Hot* went into general release and floored the movie-going public. People were in the aisles from Passaic to El Paso, and even the stodgiest of critics hailed its arrival. The film earned Oscar nominations for direction, writing, cinematography, and costume design, and Lemmon was entered for best actor. In keeping with the Academy's usual grasp of comedy, *Some Like It Hot* lost for everything except costumes, but that meant no end to the praise that was flying fast and thick. Lemmon would talk about Wilder in superlatives only, and the normally aloof director was doing some gushing of his own, explaining that Jack's "unabashed forwardness was making that preposterous situation work, elevating, removing the taint of transvestism." Wilder was ready to substantiate his confidence,

SOME LIKE IT HOT (1959). With Joe E. Brown

speaking for his script collaborator as well: "Within three to four weeks after the start of production, Diamond and I had decided that this was not to be a one shot thing with Jack. We wanted to work with him again."

The difference between shadowy Chicago and Lemmon's next film was the difference between night and Day—Doris, to be exact. Jack's allegiance went from drag to flag in the wispy, patriotic parable, *It Happened to Jane* (1959). The actual incentive had been a third chance to work with the impromptu repertory company of Quine and Kovacs; and together, the prudent trio keeps the eternally sunny Day from causing sunstroke.

The story is, at face value, an updated David and Goliath, cloaked in terms of the small-time entrepreneur versus the almighty corporate executive. Jane Osgood (Day) is the widowed mother of two, who converts her Maine waterfront home into a humble little lobster distributorship. The fledgling operation is jeopardized when the local railway freight service is abruptly eliminated, leaving the lobsters without transport. Osgood appeals to the better instincts of railroad magnate Harry Foster Malone (Kovacs), only to discover that he has none. From that point on, the two square off in a highly publicized battle royal that, by turns, threatens the hometown and the rail empire with ruin. Initially, the plucky lady seems without a ghost of a chance. Given Kovacs's portrayal, an attentively accurate stencil of Orson Welles's Harry Foster Kane, the scales appear heavily tipped in the railroad's favor. But the film also operates at a second level which pits the ordinarily invincible Day against this imperious capitalist. Mythically, it is Doris Day versus Citizen Kane, and the smart money is on Day. When the smoke clears, it is she who prevails.

Where then, does Lemmon figure in the mêlée? Mostly on the sidelines. He plays George Denham, lawyer, scoutmaster, and steadfast suitor of Jane Osgood, who holds down the homefront while she sallies forth to New York to do battle. The sober-sided but scrappy Denham is the mouthpiece for the homey values that hang in the balance of victory, and as Jane wins her tussle, so he wins Jane. The hapless and reformed Malone looks on with sympathy.

The stock Day performance of pristine optimism, momentary dejection, and stirring triumph, is salvaged by the poised professionalism of Quine, Kovacs and Lemmon. The direction is kind but never cute, affectionate without becoming affected. The film runs too long, but it does run. Kovacs's meticulous impersonation of Kane was largely lost on the press and public, though that does not seriously detract from his splenetic heavy. Lemmon, meanwhile, is relaxed and by his own choosing dispensable, content to execute his assigned scenes with verve while leaving Day to her established gamut of contrivances. He makes a likable paper tiger who can still summon courage under fire. *It Happened to Jane* gained him nothing, but neither did it cost him. As Jack saw it, "A charming picture when you could still do charming pictures."

Those who knew Billy Wilder well, knew he was not a frivolous man. He did not make empty promises. When he had whispered about a second film with Lemmon, he and I.A.L. Diamond were well into the planning stages of an exceptional, original screenplay. In light of the creative complacency of 1960 Hollywood, "revolutionary" better clues what was in store.

For Wilder, vision is the key to brilliance, and where others had looked upon Lemmon as a serviceable leading man, a sprightly character actor, or simply a winsome clown, Billy Wilder saw the articulation of an era. Here was a consummate figure of repression, a white-collar casualty: fidgety, tense, ingenuous, putty in the hands of corporate America. It is a tragicomic mode that is raised to quintessence in *The Apartment* (1960).

The general office of the Conso-

IT HAPPENED TO JANE (1959). With Doris Day and Steve Forrest

IT HAPPENED TO JANE (1959). With Doris Day

THE APARTMENT (1960). As C. C. Baxter

THE APARTMENT (1960). With Shirley MacLaine

lidated Life Insurance Company is a numbingly symmetrical honeycomb of ash-grey desks, clacking adding machines, and fluorescent light. Calvin Clinton Baxter is on his way out, and up. He is Bud to his friends, Buddy-Boy to the pack of company executives who use his West Side Manhattan apartment as a nestling spot for extramarital affairs. The arrangement is not without its inconveniences, nor its dividends, which goes far to explain why Baxter is promoted over deserving employees to the well-paying, if vague position of Second Administrative Assistant. The apartment bookings, kept with all the decorum of the Hilton, are suddenly thrown into disarray when the outwardly strait-laced head of personnel, J.D. Sheldrake, demands a disproportionate piece of the action. Acquiescence earns Buddy-Boy another promotion, but at the high price of near-nightly vagrancy and a besmirched reputation among his neighbors. Such are the wages of corporate harlotry.

The whole sleazy setup is doomed to collapse, which it finally does in almost lethal fashion with the foiled suicide of Sheldrake's jilted playmate, Fran Kubelik. Baxter, who feels a genuine affection for the woman, is outraged at the executive's cavalier treatment and indifference, and he blows the whistle on the entire operation. The cost of integrity is dismissal from Consolidated Life. But self-respect and Miss Kubelik cushion the fall from executive grace, which as it turns out is hardly a fall at all.

In this world of immoralists, where the only honorable winners are the losers, conformity is the watchword and uniformity its badge. That is the cynical motif that contours *The Apartment* and makes it a dehumanized aggregate of faceless workers, spineless bosses, and monstrous, geometrical buildings—a sort of moral cubism. With hypocrisy thriving, the romantics and idealists become passive stooges, as in Miss Kubelik's grim maxim, "Some people take, some people get took." This is the cutting satiric edge which Wilder hones and wields with surgical expertise, without apologetic sentiment or cheer to blunt the incision. Despite the stout running time, there is absolutely no textual tubbiness, least of all in the carefully chosen cast.

Recalling his cool malice in Wilder's suspenseful *Double Indemnity* (1944), Fred MacMurray makes a calmly contemptible Sheldrake. He exemplifies the malignant underside of executivism. Arrogant, egotistical, and unscrupulous, he has the colossal gall to maintain the pious facade of a suburban family man while making a science of adultery. It is a skillfully hateful characterization.

For each wolf a lamb, and Shirley MacLaine's Fran Kubelik goes to the slaughter with eyes wide and hopes shattered. As the pixyish company elevator operator, she has been slow to see past Sheldrake's smug fakery, and the eventual impact of truth leaves her so stripped of pride that suicide seems the only escape. MacLaine fills the role with a trust that corrodes into gloom at the realization that the blue-collar is the private preserve of the white-collar. The humiliation she suffers at the hands of Sheldrake is exceeded only by her defenselessness. For her, there is plainly no winning when the bosses hold all the cards.

C. C. Baxter is another festering of the same wound. He differs from Kubelik in that he perceives his powerlessness and instead of taking his life, barters it away. He seems a gutless wonder, quick to cash in on this sordid skin game for every last cent. It takes the near death of Miss Kubelik to jolt him out of his granite isolation, reminding him that his patrons deal in the hard currency of human emotion. Baxter is not sufficiently amoral or mercenary to be seduced totally by the game. He demonstrates that "no" can be the most courageous answer.

To the extent that Lemmon owns the role of Baxter, the performance is classic. No other actor could plumb the extremes of submission

THE APARTMENT (1960). With Fred MacMurray

and still retain a durable thread of self-respect. The actor in Lemmon allows him to be unsympathetic while the clown in him adds a delicate inlay of pathos. The clown input is not lost on Wilder, who fits Jack with a bowler hat beneath which the long face juts in a Chaplinesque expression of a solitary person in an impersonal world. Actually, much of Lemmon's performance is pantomime, and this pantomimed character is often at odds with the character who speaks the dialogue. It is not a linear technique, or even a patterned crosshatch, but a multiple strand of personality that frays, knots, and ultimately braids into the resolute and jobless champion of the film's end.

The Apartment is not easily categorized, other than to say that it is an undiluted Wilder allegory aided and abetted by Lemmon—in a phrase, "consolidated life." Its bleakness, density, and unrelenting theme left it with all the basic requirements for an Academy Awards snubbing. As it happened, Hollywood was in the mood for conscience-salving that year. The film received Oscars for art direction, editing, story and screenplay, direction, and needless to say, best picture. The only name sorely absent from the list was Lemmon, again nominated and again defeated, this time by Burt Lancaster's *Elmer Gantry*.

Were Jack a superstitious individual, he might have felt haunted by the knowledge that no actor had ever graduated from an Oscar for best supporting actor to one for best actor. In consolation, he was, however, that year's recipient of the much esteemed "Wilder": "I must stress that Jack Lemmon is simply incapable of giving a bad performance. He has that marvelous ability to communicate with the audience; it's something you are born with. The audience knows what's going through Jack's mind or soul—and they care." Artistry had its rewards.

So did diversity, and Jack was willing to look beyond motion pictures for more fresh material. He had found a script to his liking in a Bob Joseph adaptation of a Pierre Boulle novel, *Face of a Hero*, which had been presented with Lemmon in the fall of 1959 on television's *Playhouse 90*. Directed by John Frankenheimer, the story of an ambitious legal prosecutor who must choose between his career and a defendant's life, gave Jack a straight dose of dramatic acting denied to date in his film work. His television performance was solidly praised, encouraging him to stick with the property. Within one year, *Face of a Hero* was a play and in out of town rehearsal, rushing headlong into a December Broadway opening. Hobbled by production setbacks and a script whose drama somehow ballooned into

THE APARTMENT (1960). As C. C. Baxter

melodrama in transition to the stage, the play fell on its face. Jack opted to own up to his mistaken judgment, and rather than conjure one of the mysterious ailments that frees stars from failed shows, he captained his ship to the ocean floor—eight shows a week for twelve weeks, the Titanic with a slow leak.

Ringside defeatists were sure that Lemmon had at last sabotaged his career. Jack had an early sample of the full consequences: "The next morning after we opened there were nine reviews, eight of them stinking! Yet when I came out of my hotel room that day, there were three scripts propped against the door from producers who'd heard we'd flopped and figured I would be available soon. That's how much I got hurt." That's also how he became known as an actor of grit and principle.

On screen, Lemmon may have been evolving one of the great schnook images of his time, but off screen and out of wedlock, Jack led a full and lively existence. He continued his affair with the piano and to his supreme pleasure, recorded an album, "A Twist of Lemmon." He indulged his Winnepesaukee habit as a fisherman, and visited often with Millie, who had moved to town the year before. Not all was tame, however. A particular passion had risen above the rest; her name was Felicia Farr. Jack first met the attractive young actress through a musician friend, Freddie Kaeger, and was hopelessly smitten. But this was not to be chapter two of "The Couple Next Door." Jack was appreciably marriage shy, and Felicia, who had been married at 15 and divorced at 20, was downright phobic. As might be expected of two strong-willed, overcautious individuals, they entered into a roller-coaster relationship, as voluble as it was volatile. If tranquillity had been a bad sign in Jack's first marriage, then this newfound turbulence augured a match made in heaven.

Back at Columbia, the recent death of Harry Cohn had created a lapse in leadership. Impatient to make a show of strength, the studio slapped together a mammoth three-hour star-gazer upon which it draped the most slender of plots, and called it *Pepe* (1960). The Mexican comedian, Cantinflas, is locked into the title role and he must shoulder a burden of no fewer than twenty-eight cameos. What story there is gets trampled under foot, but that is par for the course in backlot grab bags. The nettlesome defect is the style of presentation. We don't so much see actors, singers, dancers, and personalities, as we do "celebrities," which is a polite way of saying commodities. By that logic, Lemmon accordingly appears as Daphne, because that had been his highest

With Felicia Farr

priced packaging so far. That was the mentality he was now up against at Columbia, certainly the manner of thinking that led to *The Wackiest Ship in the Army* (1961).

With Lemmon back in Navy khakis and awash in World War II South Pacific, it's just possible that the studio had hopes of doing to Ensign Pulver what MGM had sequelled to death with Andy Hardy, except that Lemmon, unlike Mickey Rooney, did not defy the laws of nature—he simply grew up.*

The title alone promises the worst, and the film fulfills the promise. From the tired premise, to the overworked gags, to the palsied action, it is the biggest nautical piracy since Blackbeard. The story, concerning a tramp schooner staffed with an inept crew and commissioned for top-secret special duty, is like a floating pawnshop of second-hand gimmicks. As if the premise were not matter enough, Ricky Nelson is laughable as the ship's ensign, never more so than with a rendition of "Do You Know What It Means to Miss New Orleans?"—a title just aching for a rejoinder. The supporting cast is no help, and the direction is a veritable flotilla of clichés. Heroically, Lemmon saves the film from the washout it so richly deserves.

*Warner Brothers actually got around to making a sequel, *Ensign Pulver* (1964), with Robert Walker.

It is an impressive and Herculean one-man show, with Lemmon in command as the skipper. He has a pleasantly seasoned look, wears his uniform with authority, takes his falls with grace, and even pumps up the valor for a battle sequence. His acting is articulate and agreeable; it is the one thing that makes *The Wackiest Ship in the Army* an underrated programmer and not an overwrought cartoon. Suffice it to say, without Lemmon, there would be no movie.

Lemmon soon showed that he was every bit as enterprising as he was dependable. With his father's expert counsel, he formed his own production company. Jalem Productions, as it was dubbed, differed from other star-bound outfits in that it did not exist for the sole promotion and sale of its patron saint. Lemmon wanted to use Jalem as an incubator for talents that might otherwise go undeveloped. This did not exclude a helpful nudge now and then, but the aim was emphatically not monopoly of Lemmon, nor even, primarily profit. Jalem's maiden film venture was to import a work by French director Albert Lamorisse, creator of the delightful short fantasy, *The Red Balloon* (1957). His *Stowaway in the Sky* (1962) is in the same lyrical vein, but drags at feature length and dulls with spotty English dubbing and a wordy narrative text by S.N. Behrman.

PEPE (1960). With Cantinflas

Lemmon's lilting narration adds considerable lift, and for its many weaknesses, *Stowaway* still makes a pleasant change from the assembly line youth items of the Disney factory.

In 1946, Alfred Hitchcock directed *Notorious*. Sixteen years later, Richard Quine directed *The Notorious Landlady* (1962), a long overdue salute to Hitchcock, Agatha Christie, and the select few who had helped make the red herring the caviar of high pulp. What makes the film more than a testimonial is that it weaves its references, pays its homage, and then spins off in its own dizzied direction. The story is simplicity swaddled in garments of devious intrigue.

Carlye Hardwicke is an American living in London. She is tried for the alleged killing of her vanished husband, but with no corpse there's no conviction and she is turned loose, a walking scandal. William Gridley is a junior American embassy official recently transferred to London and loosed on the streets, cautioned only to keep a low profile. Like clockwork, the unaware Gridley immediately sublets a room from the infamous Hardwicke, sending a mild shockwave through the consulate. Hop-

THE WACKIEST SHIP IN THE ARMY (1961).
With Ricky Nelson

ing to turn the fragile situation to advantage, Scotland Yard drafts the diplomat as an in-house spy and auxiliary corpse bloodhound. However, the more Gridley learns about his landlady, the more he is convinced of her innocence. She no sooner seems on the brink of vindication when her formerly scarce spouse appears on the scene alive and well, until an argument and ensuing scuffle leaves him shot and conclusively dead. There's a second trial, but some startling last-minute testimony by a mysterious Agatha Brown clears Hardwicke of blame. Here, the film stops snooping and starts spoofing.

The deceased husband had been holding a cache of stolen jewels which his wife knew nothing about, but about which her surprise witness knew all. That settled, there begins a riotous chase with landlady and tenant stalking the once mysterious, now murderous Brown —the actual killer of Mr. Hardwicke, among others. The last leg of the chase takes place at a seaside geriatric retreat, with a last murder averted and patients applauding, all to the strains of Gilbert and Sullivan's *The Mikado*. The film concludes, on cue, with the culprit Brown under wraps and the landlady no longer notorious.

Richard Quine's trim direction holds the lid on bafflement, while sowing the seeds of suspense. There is a rash of allusions to Miss Christie, plus a wonderfully wry bathtub sight pun on the unforgettable shower murder of Hitchcock's *Psycho* (1960). The rest is allegiance in tone, until the film cuts loose into slapstick, which, in truth, is not wholly alien to the suspense genre. The film is long-winded in the sixties fashion, although Quine covers the scattered low spots with high visual style.

As the landlady Hardwicke, Kim Novak does little more than purr and bulge and dry an occasional tear. That is essentially all the part calls for, and her talents are equal to the call. By way of defense, she does well by the closing knockabout comedy, which is one of the palpable rewards when sex goddesses show their feet of clay. Novak's only other contribution is the creation of her own wardrobe, from which it can safely be said that her sense of design is on a par with her sense of acting.

The role of the senior embassy official is handed to Fred Astaire, whose appearance is interesting for more than the taste and élan of his post-musical work. Astaire had been as much an index to his era as was Lemmon to the early sixties. They share an innocent, boyish manner, and a full complement of winces, takes, and facial tics. Each is in control of body and gesture, but in diametrically different ways. Astaire, the dancer, is flow, where Lemmon, the comic actor, is inter-

THE WACKIEST SHIP IN THE ARMY (1961).
Lieut. Crandall and his rather unusual ship's crew

THE NOTORIOUS LANDLADY (1962). With Kim Novak

ruption, although each style is part and parcel of the persona. Astaire is weightless, simple poetry; Lemmon is earthbound, complex prose. Astaire is silk to Lemmon's polyester.

In what is basically a drab part, Lemmon exhibits tremendous imagination. Like a jazz musician improvising on a simple tune, Lemmon plays his puny diplomat at a variety of rhythms, sharp in most scenes and seldom flat. He has perfected a method of telegraphing his dialogue at will, tipping his lines with an advance visual sign and then confirming, deflecting, or dodging anticipation with the delivery. This is particularly useful in scenes with Novak where Lemmon is virtually called upon to act for two, while in more supportive company, he is able to retrench for a mild, ingratiating presence. Of still greater note is Lemmon's mastery in the closing chase passage. Appended by Quine as a rollicking silent two-reeler, the segment highlights the classic ingredient of Lemmon's pantomime. Like the voice, the body can make a single statement, or a series of intertwining statements. The face is a blank page upon which the scrawl of features becomes animated and often agitated. If *It Should Happen to*

THE NOTORIOUS LANDLADY (1962). With Estelle Winwood, Kim Novak, and Fred Astaire

DAYS OF WINE AND ROSES (1962). With Lee Remick

You was Lemmon's comic matriculation, *The Notorious Landlady* was his diploma—cum laude.

An interesting footnote to the film is that it literally includes two Jack Lemmons. Jack's father had been on the west coast visiting and was talked into a walk-on as a dapper, derbied Englishman. As shooting continued, the elder Lemmon complained of flagging health and checked into a hospital for routine tests. The diagnosis was terminal cancer, and in retrospect, that further accentuates the strength of young Jack's performance.

The most creative temperaments are also the most restless. Jack's continued success with comedy only increased his appetite for something else. Once again, television was there with the spark. Cliff Robertson and Piper Laurie had recently been starred in a poignant teleplay by J. P. Miller about the harsh realities of alcoholism. There was certain to be a film version, but it was generally agreed that neither Robertson nor Laurie had the billing strength to sell so stark a drama. Jack knew beyond a doubt that he was the actor for the part. His conviction stemmed from a number of experiences, the very least of which was his smash inebriate in summer stock of '48. To begin with, he had been a lifelong observer of his mother, Millie, who, though not an alcoholic, was probably at the far limit of social drinking. And Jack, no stranger to drink himself, had had a brief bout with booze in the dreary aftermath of his divorce from Cynthia. Yet, in acting, experience alone is no guarantee of an effective performance. What really sold Jack on the role was an unflinching belief in his own dramatic potential, a belief he was impatient to share with the moviegoing public. There was one obstacle. The property was, after much delay, to be produced by Twentieth Century-Fox, but the studio had just lost its shirt on an exorbitant remake of *Cleopatra* and was in no mood or financial position to take a flyer on Lemmon. Fox put the project on the block, where it stayed for some time until the curmudgeonly Jack Warner not only gave the public *Days of Wine and Roses* (1962), but gambled on Lemmon in the lead.

Thematically, the film nearly picks up where *The Apartment* left off, with Lemmon now an advertising executive pandering to the lurid needs of his client. Where Wilder's film offered no antidote to the white-collar skin game, *Days of Wine and Roses* graphically depicts the effects of false panaceas that come in bottles.

Joe meets Kirsten, and they marry. He is essentially a man of integrity whose job forces him into daily compromise. He finds that alcohol takes the sting out of self-contempt, and she discovers that inebriety loves company. Drink becomes their bond, but the spiraling doses work to diminishing effect. Joe loses job after job as Kirsten loses touch with their young daughter. They try a passel of half-hearted remedies, but their refusal to admit to alcoholism is prohibitive to cure. Only with the excruciating aftermath of a nightmarish binge does Joe finally turn to others for help. His subsequent membership in Alcoholics Anonymous provides a methodical sobering, but also alienates him from his wife, whose drinking has worsened and led her to a tramp's life. They attempt a reconciliation, but that results in a harrowing relapse for Joe. After another torturous drying out, he must concede that the marriage will never mend unless Kirsten positively gives up drink. On that tenuous note, the film ends.

With such soul-baring material as this, acting is less problematic than overacting. In a departure from his generally frilly fare, Blake Edwards directs with a restraint that denies theatricality. At its best, the film is an environment, and Joe and Kirsten the random victims of an endemic alcoholism. This both authenticates and frames the dialogue, which might otherwise spill over into the self-conscious. However, the burden of realism is choice, knowing just what to include. Edwards chooses not to choose, and overloads the film with dramatic information. He is able to abbreviate in spots through some pointed jump cuts and one or two efficiently condensed scenes. But editing is no substitute for selectivity, and the film suffers for compression. Time passes arbitrarily and not by filmic suggestion, robbing the narrative of movement. The problem is not overacting, but an overabundance of excellent acting. *Days of Wine and Roses* would have been twice the film with half the material.

The actors are penalized by the director, though not beyond redemption. As Kirsten, Lee Remick gives full sway to her knack for the nice girl gone naughty. Her innocence at the outset inverts with drink and deteriorates into the pitiably trashy character of the picture's end. The Remick manner is a bit too stiff to sink convincingly into drunkenness, although it translates well into the tragic despair of an individual trapped in addiction.

Despite the patchy direction, Lemmon's work is masterful. There is not a molecule of Joe's body that he does not envelop, and the essence of his acting technique here is that it disappears. His Wilderesque susceptibility benefits the role, as does his own comic instinct and timing. A lush is a clown of sorts, and Lemmon is equipped to reveal just how tormented and horrified a clown is when divested

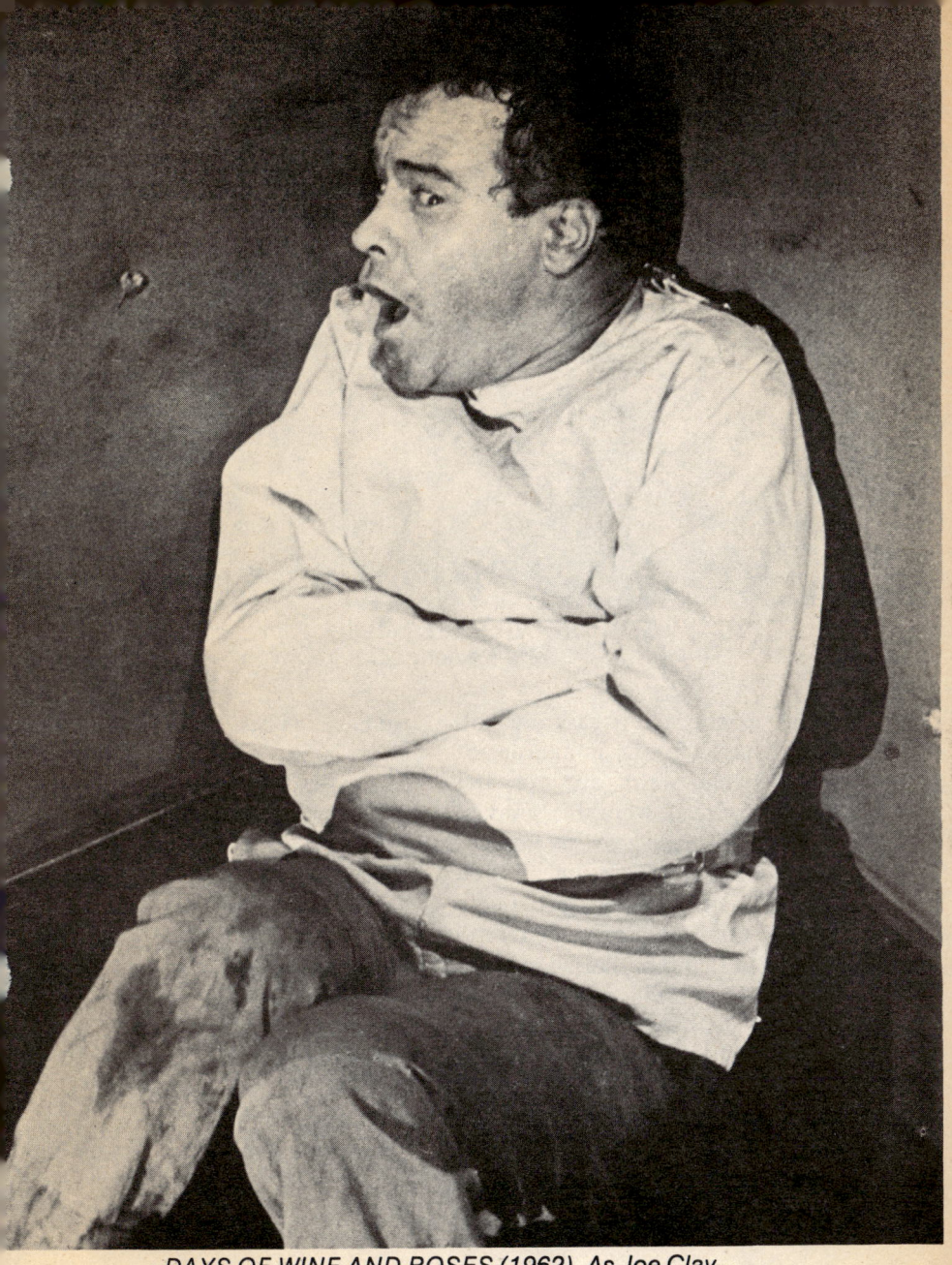

DAYS OF WINE AND ROSES (1962). As Joe Clay

DAYS OF WINE AND ROSES (1962). With Lee Remick and Katherine Squire

of his mask, in this case alcohol. His scenes of panic, in and out of the alcoholic ward, are raw and gnawingly real, while his gradual recovery through "AA" is fittingly mute, minimally pedantic. It is an indelible interpretation, jarred only by the film's intermittent bumpiness. Had Lemmon chosen to make *Days of Wine and Roses* his Broadway vehicle, he would undoubtedly have been spared the deflation of *Face of a Hero*. Theater's loss was film's gain.

Lemmon's performance was soon legend, and all the more moving when it was learned that his father had died in the course of shooting. He was once more in the running for best actor, and looked to be a heavy favorite. This time, Sidney Poitier was the spoiler, winning for his accomplished work in *Lilies of the Field*, a film whose optimistic racial message poured like honey into the hopes of sixties liberal America. Frankly, the Academy was unlikely to endorse an austere, downbeat performance that year, however brilliant the acting, when it could be congratulating itself on its own progressive-mindedness.

Lemmon could have written off the slight to bad timing, but he had seen too many old gangster pictures not to know that the three-time loser usually gets life.

There are three things an actor should do only for a trusted director: take pratfalls, improvise, and wear women's clothes. Cary Grant did all three for Howard Hawks and never had cause for regret. Jack Lemmon had done as much for Billy Wilder, and was about to tread a fourth tightrope—appear as a pimp.

It is no secret that Wilder's mocking life-view amounts to little more than variations on a theme of prostitution. So far, the director had contented himself with oblique references, but he was now ready to get down to the real thing, or as real as good taste and the law would allow. *Irma La Douce* (1963) is based on the musical by Alexandre Breffort and is a tribute to the Paris practitioners of the world's oldest profession. True to the Wilder iconoclasm, the prostitutes in *Irma La Douce* are treated with the highest ethical regard.

Apart from any lingering doubts over his role, the pre-production spell was especially hard on Lemmon. His father was not long in the grave when Felicia was called away to New York for an acting assignment. This left him alone and, to his surprise, depressed, and when the company travelled to Paris in July of 1962, his thoughts turned all the more to Felicia. By late July he was distraught. By early August she was on her way to visit. On August 15, Jack and Felicia were married.

GOOD NEIGHBOR JACK

"You are a liar, a drunk, a lech, and one of the most ridiculous men I have ever met in my life."—to Jack Lemmon as Hogan in *Under the Yum-Yum Tree*, 1963

Richard Quine and Billy Wilder were asked to do what neither had done as director, collaborate, in this case on the duties of best man. The ceremony was conducted entirely in French, by rote on Jack's part. The bride and groom exchanged the traditional vows, and afterwards tacked on a few of their own. Felicia still recites the pact, "We agreed that there would never be a divorce, no matter what. That does not mean one might not leave the other, and then maybe sneak back and murder him—but no divorce!" The newlyweds did everything but sign before officials in Geneva. By day, Jack romped with bawds, by night he honeymooned.

Irma La Douce is more about professionalism than prostitution. Life on Rue Casanova is a rigidly organized society of rules and regulated status. Lemmon plays Nestor, a naive gendarme who intrudes upon the community and momentarily upsets the system, in violation of the unspoken police policy of "live and let live." The indiscretion, such as it is, costs Nestor his job, and penniless, he is taken in by Rue Casanova's whore with a heart of gold, and an earning power to match, Irma La Douce (Shirley MacLaine). In time, Nestor becomes Irma's lover and business manager, a pair of duties his old-fashioned conscience makes difficult to mutually discharge. Hoping to reconcile the two, he decides on deception, posing both as pimp and client. The charade persists to antic proportions, as Nestor succeeds in luring Irma from her trade and delivering her to the altar perilously pregnant. The labor pains begin just moments after the ceremony begins, and it's a tossup whether she will be first a wife or a mother. Propriety wins out, as she dashes from vows to vestry for delivery, and Nestor is simultaneously reinstalled on the police force.

Leave it to Wilder to get sentimental over streetwalkers. He falls victim to the very bourgeois morality he intends to mock; seeing virtue in prurience is far less incisive than the reverse. Although the milieu is set in painstaking detail, the story is stylized to the point of triviality. It's as if Wilder sets out with Brecht in mind, and somehow is detoured through Oz. The script even has Irma scolding Nes-

IRMA LA DOUCE (1963). On the set with Shirley MacLaine and director Billy Wilder

IRMA LA DOUCE (1963). With Shirley MacLaine

tor with all the finger-waggling sanctimony of Dorothy, "You ought to be ashamed of yourself, scaring a little dog like that." In partial consequence, the direction never settles on a single vantage, bouncing from satire, to farce, to fantasy, to drama, to burlesque, and finally romance—in a word, a pastiche. That, and the epic length of two and one-half hours hints that Wilder's double duties as producer and director are working at cross purposes with the material. Admittedly, he had gone to much trouble and expense in achieving textural fidelity, but he has spared the scissors and spoiled the movie.

Another drawback is that Shirley MacLaine is given too much to do, and her Irma is caught in the crush of the film's constantly shifting perspective. At one moment she's supposed to be sassy brothel bait; at another a naive, nurturing figure; and at still another, a prim romantic ready to sacrifice all for love. Faced with such clashing character dimensions, she simply becomes a dimensionless reminder of the film's fundamental chaos.

Similarly, Lemmon is asked to cover too much territory in his characterization, but since his own surplus of nervous energy seems ever on the brink of chaos, he is better able to cope with the hectic caprices of the story. Creditable acting is out of the question, but he does survive the film admirably. And whatever the shortcomings of *Irma La Douce*, it still made money hand over fist. Lemmon may have tripped on Wilder's tightrope, but he fell into a bed of green.

What Lemmon wouldn't do for love or money, he would do for loyalty. When he heard that his co-best man, Richard Quine, would be directing a new comedy for Columbia, he signed sight unseen. To Lemmon's everlasting regret, Quine was pulled for illness and replaced by novice David Swift, whose comedy pedigree could boast but a pair of feature films for Hayley Mills. Lemmon shuddered to think he might be back in Doris Day-land.

As a rule, when a short writing grasp reaches for sophistication, it generally ends up with adolescence. *Under the Yum Yum Tree* (1963) wishes desperately to be Noël Coward, but it is strictly Lawrence Roman, never more. From the play of the same name and author, the film is a lewd little sex farce of the leering, voyeuristic school of lust. Typical of arid comic constructions, there is no story but merely an overworked situation. A virtuous college co-ed wants a sample of sex-free cohabitation with her boyfriend, hoping to gauge their compatibility and insure that, if they marry, they marry for the right reasons, the wrong reason being passion. They select a roomy apartment in which to conduct this

IRMA LA DOUCE (1963). As Nestor

experiment in living, but the landlord turns out to be an oversexed ne'er-do-well whose abiding hobby is his female tenants. The situation artlessly works through its series of combinations, each of which computes zero. By the movie's conclusion, the platonic couple is fast for the altar (for both the right and wrong reasons), and the landlord is again busily at his hobby.

Under The Yum Yum Tree is the very worst in keyhole coyness. Its lechery and innuendo have nothing to offer in the bargain by way of social comment, parody, or, for that matter, honest sexplay. The dialogue is hollow and the characters ill conceived, excluding even a semblance of stylistic flourish. The film is a very poor argument for itself.

Acting in such sludge is like moving through water, with obvious results for the leaden Dean Jones. Although this precedes his onslaught in a slew of Disney features, he is already incurably laundered and as lusty as Mickey Mouse. Repeating his stage role as David, the experimental roommate, Jones does not exactly ooze sexuality, leaving his claims of passion just so much talk. Carol Lynley is another story. Her clinical-minded Robin is fairly bursting with libidinal drive, the simple presence of which throws the movie out of kilter, since there is no worthy male on hand as ballast, Lemmon included.

As Hogan, the lecherous landlord, the reputation as an Olympian lover does not jibe with the character. Lemmon plays him as a pushy, prying philanderer, more huckster than hustler. It is an irreparably defective role, toward which Lemmon is more attentive and generous than he rightfully needs to be. It is with Hogan that author Roman grasps wildly at the urbane, only to come up with a handful of pretentious smut. In like manner, the script calls for Hogan to be dressed throughout in ravenous red; the intent is predator but the effect is of an overripe tomato. Under the yum yum tree, Lemmon withers on the vine.

In all fairness, it must be remembered that early sixties comedy was a lean field of competition. Potboiler that it is, *Under The Yum Yum Tree* still finished in the money, paying roughly ten to the million and wheedling Lemmon into another mirthless exercise. The result, *Good Neighbor Sam* (1964), is a notch above its forerunner, but, naturally, not up to Lemmon's stride.

David Swift again directs in what must be described, for want of a better term, as a "pantry" comedy. The film is set in a suburban world where manicured lawns sprawl, rectangular ranch homes squat, and life's conflicts seem as likely to tumble out of the kitchen pantry as anywhere. Sam Bissel is afflicted

UNDER THE YUM YUM TREE (1963). As Hogan

UNDER THE YUM YUM TREE (1963). With Carol Lynley and Dean Jones

with sanity; he dislikes the advertising firm where he is employed in design, and has no use for his glib, ambitious workmates. He is a private man, and he is permitted anything but privacy. At work, a top account is dumped in his lap, primarily because he has the good sense to avoid it. At home, a divorcée neighbor is dumped in his lap, because she must pretend to be properly married in order to qualify for a multi-million-dollar family legacy. Inevitably, the two duties bump heads, as Sam runs ragged pleasing everybody but himself. True to comic license, however, the commotion all funnels down to a happy ending.

Good Neighbor Sam is frightfully close to being a good movie. Swift's technique is much improved, having learned the value of the dialogue two-shot and the well-composed gag. But textually, the movie tends toward the diagrammatic, offering a blueprint in place of actual comic framework. Situations are set up and allowed to sputter. Granted, the problem of ending comedy films is as old as comedy itself, but inconclusiveness is amplified in such protracted films as *Sam* that came to replace the double bill. Swift's movie is like a combined programmer and feature that doesn't really end, it stops—forty minutes too late.

In her Hollywood debut, Austrian actress Romy Schneider supplies a certain continental elegance as the divorcée. She is fresh and exotic, something of an Anna Sten minus the Garbo fixation. On loan from television, Dorothy Provine makes a perky suburbanite Mrs. Bissel, handling the Pandora's pantry input with reserve and little of the misogynous flunkyism of, for instance, a Lucille Ball or Gracie Allen.

As scripted, Sam Bissel is like a thrice-removed C. C. Baxter. Yet Lemmon has the originality to skirt plagiarism with specificity. The character is created by the actor, and the movie rallies with his non-imitation. Sam is an eccentric individual, not an idiosyncratic dupe; his thoughts are secluded and his behavior introspective. He has a solid sense of himself and places no price tag on his convictions, but he is bighearted and liable to being finessed into untidy dilemmas. Lemmon captures the personality with a beagle expression that gawks at the world from behind horn-rimmed glasses. The intuitive clown is there, and though the portrayal is subdued, his eyebrows daintily juggle around the glasses, and his posture wears an aptly bewildered slouch. Regrettably, the script bungles the

GOOD NEIGHBOR SAM (1964). With Romy Schneider and Dorothy Provine

portrait by demanding an overdose of frantic action for a finale. And Jack thought Dagwood Bumstead had been retired to the Sunday funnies.

Good Neighbor Sam was, in kind, prey to the curse of unwarranted financial success, leading Lemmon to the final phase of a cash-trash trilogy, *How to Murder Your Wife* (1965). Jack was back with his favorite Columbia director, but a fifth of Quine should have been sufficiently filling. This sixth teaming is one trip to the well too many.

Hyperbole, the method of comment through exaggeration, is a lot like cracking walnuts with a sledge hammer—the means obliterates the end. More screenwriters get used by hyperbole than use it, and George Axelrod is a case in point. He is often so taken with technique that he forgets what it is he has to say, assuming he has anything to say in the first place. That is what's the matter with Axelrod, and Axelrod is what's the matter with *How to Murder Your Wife*. What begins as a snide little male fable about the pernicious perils of marriage sours into a grouchy vendetta against women. It's not entirely apparent whether the motive is armchair malice or male menopause, but the effect is the same.

The plot, or better, the conspiracy, unfolds with the liquor-induced marriage of Stanley Ford, popular cartoonist and heretofore unbudging bachelor. The bride is a blonde, voluptuous Italian who, as is discovered, speaks not a word of English. Were Axelrod a run-of-the-mill male chauvinist, he might have contented himself with this mute plaything as his idea of the perfect spouse. But his venom knows no such bounds. Instead, the woman is depicted as yet another agent of the international conspiracy of wedlock, which Axelrod would have us believe is nothing more than a hammerlock with in-laws. There is an outlandish contrivance, as Ford, who carries out a vicarious wife execution in his cartoon strip, is arrested for murder when his wife actually vanishes. Insult is added in jury when an all-male panel delivers a verdict of "not guilty", as much as to say that betrothal alone is grounds for justifiable homicide. Of course, the scene is hyperbole, but no less foul for that fact. Even though the script hedges by reuniting the Fords in a final, blissful embrace, there is no escaping the unsavory aftertaste of what has gone before.

All else worsens with the screenplay. Quine's direction is as disorderly as the story, with careless composition, unimaginative camera perspective, and none but the most tedious camera movement. If he has any opinion of the screenplay, it can only be inferred as silent ratification or benign ne-

GOOD NEIGHBOR SAM (1964). With Romy Schneider

glect.

Denied the luxury of anonymity, the cast becomes the real receptacle of the writer's paranoia. As the chief counseling harpy, Claire Trevor is made to appear vain, messy, greedy, and oversexed. Virna Lisi, the walking pasta who ensnares Ford and becomes Trevor's obedient helpmate, is left mindless and peculiarly mechanical for one of so ample shape. Terry-Thomas, Ford's butler and fellow misogynist, is merely warmed-over Eric Blore. Lemmon, inescapably, is bound hand and foot by the diffusely sketched character of Ford. The movie is simply too far gone for even his formidable recuperative powers.

Take a rudimentary turn-of-the-century melodrama, throw in large chunks of slapstick, add a measure of derring-do, a pinch of romance, season lightly with panoramic scenery, and simmer for 150 minutes, and you have, not a flavorful vintage stew, but a disagreeable gruel that is likely as not to cause indigestion. That is what director Blake Edwards ladles out in *The Great Race* (1965). Lemmon, a mere two days out of the frying pan of *How to Murder Your Wife*, was fast in the fire.

Tony Curtis is The Great Leslie, Lemmon his arch-rival, Professor Fate, and they compete in an automobile race from New York to Paris via a circuitous but relatively dry Siberian route. Natalie Wood is the pert Maggie DuBois (not to be confused with "Blanche") who latches on for reportage, and later, love. Along the way, they encounter mayhem, a cuddlesome polar bear, a gargantuan pie fight, and a lunatic crown prince who bears more than a passing resemblance to Fate. In time, it ends, then upends, allowing for a sequel. It cost $12 million to make.

The Great Race doesn't do much that couldn't have been done better and cheaper with a banana peel and Buster Keaton. But Edwards is not to be denied his extravagance. Among the waste is Curtis, who did far better as Josephine; Lemmon, who did far better as Daphne and a dozen others; and Peter Falk, who is capable of far better work. Natalie Wood is Natalie Wood.

Fortunately, Billy Wilder was still Billy Wilder, and he had just the tonic for Jack's sagging film health. "It's about greed, love, compassion, human understanding," outlined the director, who of late, had been hounded by censors, "but not about sex." No sex, just an off-key hymn to insurance fraud.

The Fortune Cookie (1966) tells of Harry Hinkle, a network sports cameraman who suffers a minor concussion while covering a professional football game in Cleveland. He regains consciousness in a hospital ward, only to find that his vulturous lawyer brother-in-law,

HOW TO MURDER YOUR WIFE (1965). As Stanley Ford

HOW TO MURDER YOUR WIFE (1965). With Virna Lisi

THE GREAT RACE (1965). With Tony Curtis and Natalie Wood

Willie Gingrich, has swooped in with lawsuits bulging from every pocket. Hinkle is suckered into wheel-chair imposture, as Gingrich sets to work and the immediate parasitic world moves in for a portion of the insurance pie. From his sedentary perspective, Hinkle witnesses both the unrepentant greed of his fellow man, and the guilt-stricken degeneration of Boom-Boom Jackson, the football player whose inadvertent sideline collision set the whole collusion into motion. With the boodle well within reach, Hinkle has a change of heart, stages a miraculous recovery, and makes amends with Jackson in a touching pigskin apology played before a vacant Municipal Stadium.

It was obvious from the outset that Gingrich was the film's plum role. Walter Matthau, who, despite unassailable stage credentials, had been playing short end parts in a dozen and a half screen outings, was astonished that a top draw like

THE GREAT RACE (1965). With Tony Curtis

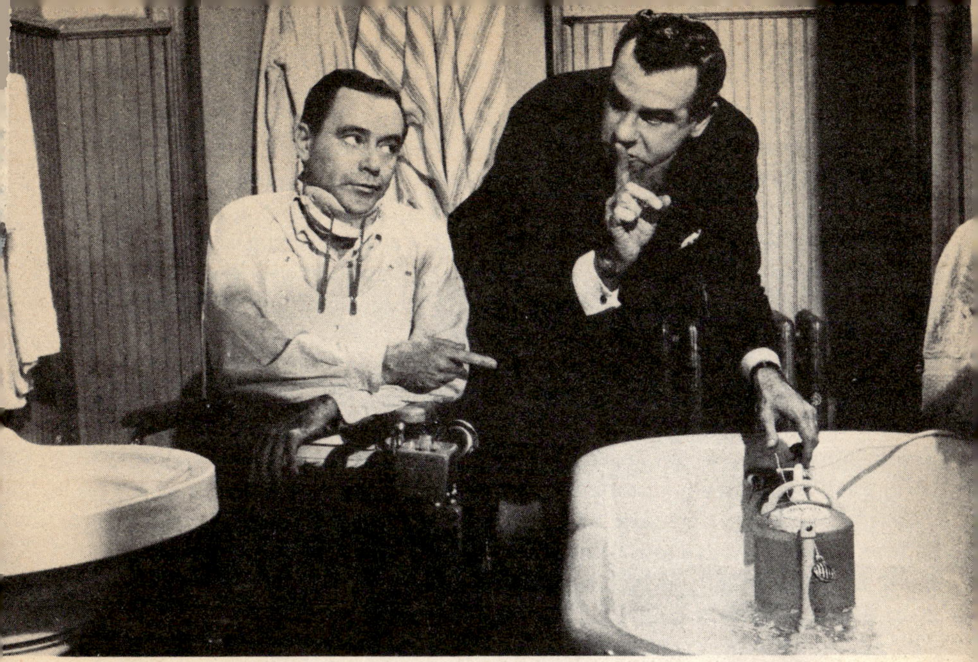

THE FORTUNE COOKIE (1966). With Walter Matthau

THE FORTUNE COOKIE (1966). With Ron Rich

Lemmon was unselfishly passing up the script's best material. Jack, a fan of Matthau's for years, knew that the actor deserved better than he had received in the past. The two men were not friends before the production, but they were fast friends afterwards. As the shyster lawyer Gingrich, Matthau is flawless. He is an undiluted amoralist with an instinct for the jugular, the ironic epitome of a Wilder antihero, a self-honest dishonest man.

With Hinkle, Lemmon and Wilder break new ground. Where *Some Like It Hot* refined Jack's extraordinary craft as a comic actor, *The Fortune Cookie* revealed that he was the best straight man in contemporary Hollywood. What is it Lemmon does? He doesn't. He doesn't upstage Matthau, he doesn't step on others' lines, he doesn't place his own humor above the film's. The classic Lemmon timing is in full flower, down to the last beat. Although "chemistry" is a label critics toss about when they're at a loss to analyze particulars, it is still the best description of the way Lemmon and Wilder were able to brew new cinematic solutions.

Shooting on *The Fortune Cookie* endured a telling setback when Matthau suffered a major coronary. The production marked time for seven weeks while the actor convalesced, and the Lemmons passed the time spoiling their new daughter, Courtney Noel. The delay did not crimp the film's impact. Matthau was named the year's best supporting actor. The Academy was not awarding an Oscar for best straight man that year, but had it been, the resurrected Lemmon would have easily walked off with it in his hip pocket.

Art does not exist in a vacuum, least of all popular art. With America's agonizing involvement in Viet Nam, the country was coming of age, and with it, guardedly, Hollywood as well. Motion pictures were at last ready for Jack Lemmon.

The public officially registered its readiness for Lemmon, making him 1967's top box-office draw, a tangible trophy he used for creative, not economic leverage. Jack's first act of freedom was to appear in a film adaptation of Murray Schisgal's surprise Broadway success, *Luv*. The play takes the abysmal existentialism of the then dominant avant-garde theater, and turns it on its head. By running three characters through the vocabulary of modern day alienation, he shows that the only thing more absurd than life is the self-serious merchant of gloom and despair. The intelligent response to society is not paranoia, as comedian Lenny Bruce announced, but a sense of humor.

The play loses much in translation to film. To begin with, Clive Donner's direction lacks the surreal-superreal sensibilities that Mike Nichols brought to the stage production. Then, Elliott Baker's screenplay is a scissors-and-paste affair that parcels the dialogue over expanded segments and loads the text with unnecessary characters and tacky transitional graphics.

VINTAGE LEMMON

"I'm a neurotic nut, but you're crazy."—as Felix Ungar in *The Odd Couple*, 1968

Last, and fatally overlooked, American film's avant-garde is not comparable to the theater's, leaving the satire without a contextual leg to stand on. *Luv* (1967) sways and topples.

It is still a fascinating failure for which the cast cannot be faulted. Peter Falk and Elaine May are weasel and tigress as Milt and Ellen Manville. Lemmon is sallow and sickly as the suicidal Harry Berlin, but because of the screenplay's inadequacies he impresses as inane instead of wantonly insane, as intended. The film's only improvement over the play is a mood-setting score by jazz musician Gerry Mulligan.

Jack was stalled but not stymied. He lowered his sights to less lofty play-to-film fare and accepted the role of Felix in *The Odd Couple* (1968). This time, the production put its best foot forward and hired the original playwright, Neil Simon, to transcribe a screenplay. The payoff is a film that rivals the play's pace and hilarity.

Felix Ungar is a likable, neurotic nebbish whose marriage of twelve years has turned to rubble. He turns to his good friend and poker companion, Oscar Madison, a divorced

LUV (1967). As Harry Berlin

LUV (1967). With Elaine May

THE ODD COUPLE (1968). With Walter Matthau

Art does not exist in a vacuum, least of all popular art. With America's agonizing involvement in Viet Nam, the country was coming of age, and with it, guardedly, Hollywood as well. Motion pictures were at last ready for Jack Lemmon.

The public officially registered its readiness for Lemmon, making him 1967's top box-office draw, a tangible trophy he used for creative, not economic leverage. Jack's first act of freedom was to appear in a film adaptation of Murray Schisgal's surprise Broadway success, *Luv*. The play takes the abysmal existentialism of the then dominant avant-garde theater, and turns it on its head. By running three characters through the vocabulary of modern day alienation, he shows that the only thing more absurd than life is the self-serious merchant of gloom and despair. The intelligent response to society is not paranoia, as comedian Lenny Bruce announced, but a sense of humor.

The play loses much in translation to film. To begin with, Clive Donner's direction lacks the surreal-superreal sensibilities that Mike Nichols brought to the stage production. Then, Elliott Baker's screenplay is a scissors-and-paste affair that parcels the dialogue over expanded segments and loads the text with unnecessary characters and tacky transitional graphics.

VINTAGE LEMMON

"I'm a neurotic nut, but you're crazy."—as Felix Ungar in *The Odd Couple*, 1968

Last, and fatally overlooked, American film's avant-garde is not comparable to the theater's, leaving the satire without a contextual leg to stand on. *Luv* (1967) sways and topples.

It is still a fascinating failure for which the cast cannot be faulted. Peter Falk and Elaine May are weasel and tigress as Milt and Ellen Manville. Lemmon is sallow and sickly as the suicidal Harry Berlin, but because of the screenplay's inadequacies he impresses as inane instead of wantonly insane, as intended. The film's only improvement over the play is a mood-setting score by jazz musician Gerry Mulligan.

Jack was stalled but not stymied. He lowered his sights to less lofty play-to-film fare and accepted the role of Felix in *The Odd Couple* (1968). This time, the production put its best foot forward and hired the original playwright, Neil Simon, to transcribe a screenplay. The payoff is a film that rivals the play's pace and hilarity.

Felix Ungar is a likable, neurotic nebbish whose marriage of twelve years has turned to rubble. He turns to his good friend and poker companion, Oscar Madison, a divorced

LUV (1967). As Harry Berlin

slob of a sports writer who lives in high-rent squalor on Riverside Drive in Manhattan. The two become temporary roommates, and within days, each is at the other's throat. Their marriage of convenience is instantly on the rocks, as the compulsively finicky Felix neatens and sanitizes Oscar's unkempt domain. The friction comes to a head, and Felix decides to go it alone, although the two are closer and wiser for having endured the other's (and through that their own) obnoxiousness.

Gene Saks's direction is clean and crisp, and wisely opens up on the atmosphere of the West Side. The dialogue is well staged and buoyed by a modest visual component of quick takes and tight physical gags. The remarkably rounded supporting cast is shuffled with authority and hurried off camera without pause for Felix and Oscar's central byplay.

In an encore to his acclaimed stage performance, the jowly Walter Matthau growls and wisecracks as Oscar Madison. A former coach himself, Matthau plays the sports-obsessed Madison from the inside out, sifting the character for every last speck of slovenly single-mindedness. This is a man for whom marriages come and go, but triple plays and winning poker hands come all too seldom.

Lemmon, in turn, wears Ungar like a fitted, permapressed suit, and the characterization scarcely sags or creases. Simon had the good judgment to stretch the role filmically, especially in a prologue enacted behind the opening credits in which Lemmon capsulizes Ungar before a word of the play is recited. All told, he is a pesky and petty defeatist, but a well-meaning companion. He is the kind of nuisance his friends would love to kill, if they didn't love him so much. Lemmon is at his finest nose to nose with Matthau where he refrains from prissiness, which might carry misleading homosexual overtones, and depicts an irritating homebody, prowling about and sporting a stubborn streak of cowardice. Felix is a retentive introvert to Oscar's expulsive extrovert, reminding us that opposites can impact as well as attract.

If the reunion of Lemmon and Matthau is *The Odd Couple*'s best feature, Simon's screenplay is still the star. There is no excess wordplay or surplus gagging; each joke advances the plot, every flurry of banter deepens the characterizations. Simon had long since come to know that plays which whir like laugh machines inevitably sputter and stop by the second act. *The Odd Couple* is a complete work, one of the few sixties comedies that promises to stand the test of time.

Lemmon was wrong to think that charming little movies had entered extinction. Just how wrong is the measure of just how charming *The April Fools* (1969) is. It is a film that, given the stormy political and social climate of the time, had every reason to pass unseen. For those very reasons, audiences took to it like a quilt on a cold night. *

Two kindred spirits come together at an ultrachic New York penthouse party. Neither could care less about high-powered life at the top; both would rather be happy than hip. They spend an enchanted night together and by morning accept that they are one another's salvation. They agree to escape by plane to Paris, and have only till that evening's departure time to disengage from obligations. He walks out on a new promotion at the office and a neurotically indifferent wife at home. She prepares to leave her unfaithful husband, but the split becomes somewhat sticky when they both discover that her new lover was once employed by her husband. There is a mad, crosscut dash to the airport and, this being a fairy tale, love wins out by a hairbreadth.

But this is a highly polished and sophisticated fairy tale, owing largely to an adult yet whimsical screenplay by Hal Dresner. The dialogue is lively and intelligent, tender and sparse in the clinch. Like most simple tales, there is a bouquet of budding meanings and metaphors there for the plucking. The story is most concise in its minor characters. Sally Kellerman's wife is a clenched suburban nightmare. Jack Weston and Harvey Korman's white-collar commuters are a double dose of backroom bravado. Peter Lawford's high-tone philandering husband is vanity in pinstripes. And Charles Boyer and Myrna Loy's sublimely screwy couple is a page out of a storybook.

Against this finely etched character backdrop, Jack Lemmon and Catherine Deneuve glow as the star-crossed lovers. At first glance, it seems an improbable match, but together they catch a special light. After years of wrestling with big-breasted kewpie dolls, Lemmon has found a fitting filmmate. He is able to diffuse Deneuve's ethereal luster, and she is able to smooth the rough corners of his modernity. Fully clothed, their shy infatuation is more erotic than a score of heaving, sweaty, movie sexfests.

The April Fools also marks the fifteen-year reunion of Lemmon and Lawford, again vying for the favors of the same woman. Aside from a touch of grey at the temples, Lawford has changed very little since *It Should Happen to You*, which is to his credit as a character actor. His stasis makes a yardstick for Lemmon's progress, and the

---

* Lemmon had his own reasons for a change of pace, with the upsetting death of Millie earlier that year.

distance is astounding. Where Jack was tinny and tense before, he is now resonant and relaxed. Many of the mannerisms remain but they are firmly controlled by his acting, not in control of it. There is still a distinct style and stamina, but, no longer dominant, it is submerged in the larger portrait. The difference is that between a character actor and an actor.

When writers set out to write the most of something, they often as not write that something to death. Neil Simon set out to write the victim comedy to end all victim comedies, and ended up with a chafing, ugly, and flirtingly sadistic screenplay. *The Out-of-Towners* (1970), about a suburban Ohio couple who considers moving to New York City for promotion reasons, is a twenty-four-hour travelogue of Manhattan on the fritz. Strike begets strike, mugging begets kidnapping, and so on in mock biblical fashion, until Simon has at last wrought his urban apocalypse. It is a comedy of errors that's dangerously light on the comedy, a grating exertion of an already abrasive wit.

Jack Lemmon and Sandy Dennis play the ill-fated visitors, and they can do little more than wriggle, quiver, and rave as Simon sinks his comic probes. It is as close to comedic vivisection as an audience is liable to see: Lemmon shrill and shrieking adenoidally, Dennis, nasal and whining incessantly. The truly fatal stroke to this perfectly wicked film is Arthur Hiller's direction. He virtually escalates the pain of it all through the rafters with perplexing hand-held shots, fish-eye lenses, and mercilessly scrutinizing close-ups. The low point of this directorial botch is an early morning fragment shot in Central Park, in which the camera actually manages to catch the tip of the boom mike in an upper corner of the frame. And that is very much to the point, since Lemmon and Dennis were not really filmed, they were framed.

Lemmon might have been disappointed, if he had had enough time, but he was too busy touching all the media bases. Before *The Out-of-Towners* was even released, he was back toiling on television. He agreed to narrate an environmental documentary for KNBC in Los Angeles, a hard-hitting exposé by Don Widener called "The Slow Guillotine." The audience response was overwhelming, and the program was instrumental in rooting an ecological awareness in the public and Lemmon alike.

There was also a stint on stage, as Lemmon accepted the part of Harry Van in Los Angeles' Ahmanson Theatre revival of the 1936 Robert Sherwood Pulitzer Prize play, *Idiot's Delight*. The performance was heartily received, which meant that by 1970 Lemmon had

THE ODD COUPLE (1968). With Walter Matthau

sampled and succeeded in almost every compartment of show business except juggling, water ballet, and motion picture direction. The first two could wait.

An old friend and business associate, Richard Carter, decided to try his hand at film production, and bought the rights to a Katherine Topkins novel about an elderly man's search for pride and identity. The property was too wholesome for the dollar-minded studios and finally out of frustration, Carter sent the script to Lemmon for an objective opinion. Lemmon not only liked it, he wanted to direct it. The deal was made and Fredric March was signed for the leading role. Now studios recoiled from what was taken to be a triple threat: an untested producer, an actor turned director, and a lead who, though one of the most distinguished actors in the trade, was no longer a box-office draw. If the project was ever to get off the ground, someone else had to be found for the old man. March gracefully bowed out, and, startling all, 50-year-old Walter Matthau offered to become 70 for the film. With that as security, ABC Pictures agreed to finance the production for a stingy $1.6 million. Carter figured a shoestring operation was better than none at all, and *Kotch* (1971) was born as a

THE APRIL FOOLS (1969). With Peter Lawford

cooperative effort. Friends and relatives were conscripted into production positions, and Felicia was signed to play Matthau's expectant daughter-in-law.

Lemmon was every bit the workhorse behind the camera as he had been in front of it. He struck a quick professional rapport with his cameraman, Richard Cline, and his editor, Ralph Winters, and in a mood of support and respect, they produced a film with more verve and technical polish than a good third of the big-budgeted pictures Lemmon had to his acting credit. *Kotch* did respectable business and, although high-hatted by a number of fashionably cynical critics, it was nominated for Oscars in four categories (including best actor), winning in none but earning the congratulations of all. Among the many rewards was one Lemmon hadn't counted on. He was becoming a superior actor for having been an adequate director. The proof was his next performance in Melville Shavelson's sleeper, *The War Between Men and Women* (1972).

Based on the life and work of cartoonist-humorist James Thurber, the film is a unique melding of harsh wit and quirky slapstick, with an equally novel blend of film and animation. Like Thurber, Lemmon's Peter Wilson must contend with rapidly deteriorating eyesight in a world he views as barely sublimated warfare. His acid personality refuses to accept imminent blindness with even an iota of self-pity, and he walls himself off from others in whom he detects the least trace of sympathy. He somehow drifts into marriage with a loopy divorcée (Barbara Harris) and overnight finds himself waist-deep in the enemy terrain of wives, children, and dogs. But the kids and the canine prove to be a likable collection of neurotics and, as paranoia loves company, Wilson endures. However, the last traumas of vision loss send him into a bitter retreat from which he caustically relents at the film's uncompromised conclusion.

The War Between Men and Women is a steely piece of comic misanthropy. Greying and handsome, Lemmon offers a letter-perfect portrait of comically skeptical disgruntlement. His voice is throaty and sarcastic, his scorn at once believable and bluff. Harris's betrothed is a literate but balmy foil, and the supporting cast is carefully shaded, with standout work from Jason Robards Jr. and Herb Edelman. The ungimmicky optical effects and the select use of subjective camera and sound, engenders a rare dynamic unity, both real and surreal. There is no other film quite like it.

If Lemmon's early career was marked by studio-imposed mediocrity and narrowness, his later film work was dedicated to newness, and

THE APRIL FOOLS (1969). With Catherine Deneuve

in the seventies, that sooner or later meant nudity. As was only fitting, this Lemmon first occurred in a Billy Wilder film; but firm or wrinkled, there must be something more to a production than an actor's behind. It's indicative of *Avanti!* (1972) that Lemmon's posterior is practically the film's most memorable aspect, the problem being that the producer Wilder is again more in evidence than the director. The film, about a pair of strangers who learn that their parents have maintained an annual affair on the Italian resort island of Ischia, is saturated with scenic footage, overattentive to the local color, and slack by a good thirty minutes. The screenplay, from the uninspired Samuel Taylor play, has several Wilder touches, like a macabre corpse kidnapping, but by and large, the crackling dialogue and gallows wit that is Wilder's signature is heavily watered down in *Avanti!*

As the strangers who first clash, then come to imitate their folks' trysting habits, Jack Lemmon and Juliet Mills are less than compelling. Lemmon plays an irascible,

THE OUT-OF-TOWNERS (1970). As George Kellerman

blue-blooded bully whose initial reaction to discovering the real motive behind his father's yearly retreats is shock. The character is so starchy and bumptious that it's difficult to accept his gradual seduction by the island and the mistress's daughter. As the daughter, Mills is dowdy and pudgy. Having been fattened for the role, she looks like a Sherman tank in chiffon. The eventual truce between the characters is not without warmth and sensuality, neither of which is Wilder's forte, and as might be expected of an astringent wit that does not play to its strength, the affair grows tepid and mushy. Wilder, now sixty-six, seemed to be losing some of his bite. Lemmon turned to untested talents.

"I should've been a ballplayer. I could've been with Brooklyn. Chicago, anyway." But it's the 1970's and the Dodgers have long since migrated to Los Angeles. So has Harry Stoner, only he's in the fashion garment business. How long he'll stay in business is another question. "Capri Casuals" is a line of sportswear that the high-living Harry has financially overextended. He can alter his life style, go bust, or burn down one of his factories for the insurance money. Harry's partner, Phil Greene, wants the business to stand or fall on its own merits, live or die by the rules, but Harry hotly counters, "There are no more rules, just referees. You want logic, Phil, and there is no ministry of logic in this country." After a series of seamy meetings with a businesslike arsonist, Harry decides to take the crooked route. We never see the purchased fire, but that would only be an anticlimax after having watched the charred remains of Harry's psyche smolder and smudge in a convoluted world.

Jack Lemmon is Harry Stoner. *Save the Tiger* (1973) is directed by John G. Avildsen from a screenplay by Steve Shagan, based on his novel. The script was written before Lemmon was signed, so it can be no more than a propitious fluke that Lemmon's nickname in *Irma La Douce* was Tiger, or that the Lemmon persona was in need of new extension and relevance around the time he was offered the part. But excellence is the interplay of talent, luck, and timing, and *Save the Tiger* has no shortage of any of these.

What Shagan has in mind is a post-Darwinist post-mortem. His metaphor, the tiger, is conspicuous but no less to the point, and if there is any residual doubt as to the implied message, it is spelled out in dialogue by a minor character, "Lions and tigers always return to a remembered place of beauty. That's how they catch them." Harry Stoner is a vulnerable man, most vulnerable in his elaborate memories. But Shagan is no

Nietzsche, and if he makes noises about the fetters of institutionalized morality or disrupted natural selection, he is really lamenting the end of professionalism, of initiative, and above all, the end of style. It is an appeal for human ecology, a plea to save the Harry Stoners who remember when music used to swing, when wars were patriotic, when baseball pitchers knew how to crank up for a fastball. It's no accident that a barroom television airs a clip from *High Sierra* (1941), where Humphrey Bogart, as a gangster fugitive from a lost romantic era, is gunned down by police snipers. Harry Stoner is an anachronism nearing the vanishing point on a horizon where the only professionals left are prostitutes and arsonists.

Save the Tiger is morbid romanticism with a downbeat ending, and studios didn't want to touch it. The property floated for some time before Paramount consented to back it, and then only for a scant one million dollars. But Lemmon had already seen the script, and convinced that it was a film that needed to be made, he traded his

THE OUT-OF-TOWNERS (1970). With Sandy Dennis

On the set as director of KOTCH (1971), with Walter Matthau

THE WAR BETWEEN MEN AND WOMEN (1972).
With Barbara Harris and Moosie Drier

customary fee for an anticipated percentage of the gross, working in the meantime for scale at $165 per week. Lemmon's conviction registers in every frame of his performance. The physical Lemmon is meticulously at work, giving Stoner color and credibility where there is danger of type and caricature. He walks in an agitated, heavy heel-toe fashion, as if the earth might fall away between each stride. He dresses and speaks with taste and authority, but his face has a hint of five o'clock shadow that looks like thin greasepaint on a sad clown.

Shagan both magnifies and focuses the Lemmon image that Billy Wilder midwifed in *The Apartment* and later orphaned in *Avanti!* Stoner's materialism is actually degrees of compromise, with self-respect teetering all the while. The character wears his prosperity, his swimming pool, his Tudor-style home, his limousine, his daughter in school in Switzerland. Then, Lemmon the actor buckles with the stress of it all, and peels back the layers of veneer until only a scarred and rotting grain remains. Bolstered by Avildsen's

THE WAR BETWEEN MEN AND WOMEN (1972).
With Barbara Harris

AVANTI! (1972). With Juliet Mills

AVANTI! (1972). With Juliet Mills

keenly detailed realism, the performance rings with an authenticity that, in turn, sustains the screenplay's more stylized impulses. Stoner is a mid-ground seventies artifact that only Lemmon could have articulated.

Lemmon was nominated a fourth time as best actor, but this time his own conduct threatened to preempt winning. A week before the awards ceremonies, there was a live, televised tribute to James Cagney. Lemmon, Jimmy's old hoofing student, was one of the scheduled speakers, but he was due for some minor surgery the next day and was on prescribed medication. While waiting his turn at the rostrum, he carelessly sipped a few glasses of wine and the chemistry was boggling. When called upon, he was discursive and his remarks became an elliptical jumble. At length, he stopped and returned to his table, where he and Felicia had words, and she responded by dousing him with a glass of water. A photographer caught it all, and the soggy sequence was splashed over every tabloid in the country. It seemed Lemmon had choked off his chances for the Oscar, especially in light of that year's competition: Marlon Brando, Al Pacino, Jack Nicholson, and Robert Redford. One week later, he was holding the elusive little statue and fumbling for words in front of a national television audience, "I had a speech prepared—in 1959. There has been a lot of controversy over this award, but I think it's one hell of an honor and I am thrilled."

It was a tough act to follow, let alone top, but Billy Wilder came up with an ideal encore, a remake of the popular classic, *The Front Page* (1974), with Jack once again in cahoots with Walter Matthau. It made sense from every angle. The durable play by Ben Hecht and Charles MacArthur was a twice-filmed proven quantity that would give Lemmon a breather, Matthau a chance to stay in the public eye, and Wilder the opportunity to settle a score of his own for those who thought his prickly wit was going to seed.

The Front Page is set in 1920's Chicago, in the press room of the city's Criminal Court Building. The hard-boiled regulars of the working press are on hand to cover the politically jockeyed hanging of a convicted murderer. The town's premier crime reporter, Hildy Johnson, picks this moment to walk out on his double-dealing editor, a renowned fourflusher and journalistic con-artist named Walter Burns. The grand exit is upstaged by the eleventh hour escape of the murderer, a jittery milquetoast who practically lands in the reporter's arms. Johnson's professional instincts get the better of him, as Burns inveigles coverage of the event as the reporter's journalistic

SAVE THE TIGER (1973). As Harry Stoner

SAVE THE TIGER (1973). With Jack Gilford

With his Oscar for SAVE THE TIGER

swan song. The ensuing commotion, exhausting by any standards, gives Burns all the opening he needs to sink his hooks back into the star reporter. When the madness finally ebbs, Johnson thinks he is on his way out, but Burns knows better.

The production is not quite up to Howard Hawks's screwball version, *His Girl Friday* (1940), with Cary Grant as Walter Burns and Rosalind Russell as Hildy Johnson (one sex change that really worked), but it isn't meant to be. This *Front Page* is an unblemished professional walk-through that does the material justice, and that is all the tribute that need be paid.

Producer Paul Monash has kept the film down to comedy fighting weight, 105 minutes, and the action percolates best in this compact pot. Beyond which, the film accomplishes precisely what it intended to: Lemmon had his leisure, Matthau his limelight, and Wilder his reputation back.

If anybody who'd seen Neil Simon's *Out-of-Towners* had heard about his *Prisoner of Second Avenue* (1975), odds are they would think twice about going. Many did, many had, and many didn't go. *Prisoner* deserved better than guilt by association: it is not an original screenplay, but a transcription of

THE FRONT PAGE (1974). With Carol Burnett

THE FRONT PAGE (1974). With Walter Matthau

Simon's own hit play; Melvin Frank is not Arthur Hiller, but a former screenwriter whose direction has a writer's regard for the text; Anne Bancroft is not Sandy Dennis, but an actress of considerable power and satirical prowess; and finally, Jack Lemmon is not Jack Lemmon underdirected and overwrought, but Jack Lemmon acting the pants off a very complex role.

Mel and Edna are a middle-class, middle-aged, middle-happy couple, who like Job, are suddenly treated to life's backside. Mel loses his job, their apartment is robbed, Edna goes to work, Mel loses his mind, Edna loses her job. Not to mention the usual niggling problems of noisy neighbors, nosey relatives, and exact bus fare. What's different about this film is that Mel and Edna absorb blow after blow, and when they seem on the verge of surrender, they thumb their noses defiantly and dig the trenches for battle. *Prisoner* is not a comedy per se, but a conspiracy of calamities where the smile is the only tether to sanity.

Lemmon avenges his mistreatment at the hands of *The Out-of-Towners*. Mel is volatile but not

THE PRISONER OF SECOND AVENUE (1975).
As Mel

*THE PRISONER OF SECOND AVENUE (1975).
With Anne Bancroft*

monotonous, a nice guy suffering urban battle fatigue. The outward symptoms are manic-depression, then despair, and finally nervous collapse. Once those trifles are out of the way, a prelude to psychosis, Mel is ready to face the music. Lemmon's anger as Mel may lapse into melancholy but it never leaps into hysteria. He is able to straddle the fine line between courage and dementia, and thereby gives full voice to Simon's paradoxical slogan of endurance. Lemmon resists resolving the conflicts that Simon has left unresolved, and that is testimony to both his nuance and reserve as an actor.

Anne Bancroft could well be Lemmon's best leading lady. Her quiet strength contains his nervous energy. She, too, is master of the straight line, and in fact nearly surpasses Lemmon as a straight man. The effect is intriguing, as though they were both George Burns and New York City was Gracie Allen. Bancroft's technique is embedded in her characterization of Edna, a wry, compassionate, sinewy woman

On television in THE ENTERTAINER, March 10, 1976

with a survivor's instincts. She less speaks her lines than chews them with a mint condition Bronx jawbone. If *Prisoner of Second Avenue* has any coherent message, it is that prison is only a state of mind, and Bancroft's Edna is the soul that defies incarceration. She and Lemmon combine in a new American Gothic—liberated, neurotic, and invincible.

With two Oscars in hand, a directorial credit, notable work on stage and in television, and even a record album, Lemmon's triumphs seemed to dwarf the remaining challenges. He accepted the role of broken-down vaudeville comic Archie Rice in a television film from the John Osborne play, *The Entertainer*. But while the production was respectable and his performance superb, the film wrongly tried to transplant this incontrovertibly British

A gathering of Oscar winners with their awards
(from the top, left to right: Sidney Poitier, Ben Johnson, Karl Malden,
Jack Lemmon, Shelley Winters, Ginger Rogers, Laurence Olivier,
Maximilian Schell, Peter Ustinov, Eva Marie Saint, Walter Matthau,
Rod Steiger, Claire Trevor, Harold Russell, Red Buttons,
and Patty Duke (Astin)

play in a mainstream American setting. Like a cowboy in Coventry, it just doesn't jibe. At fifty, and back on television, Jack was reminded that there were limits to experimentation. But he was not one to come full circle, not without actor's vertigo.

Creativity, like water, does not stand still, it stagnates. With television ever hungry at the door, Hollywood had maintained a play-safe stance that meant fewer gambles and more formulized films. Meanwhile, network television, whose career was only as old as Lemmon's, had dropped all pretense of merit and become a commercial battlefield of ratings and corporate whiz-kids who wouldn't know dramatic or comedic quality if it reared up and kicked them in their network dossier.

The popular creative world was fast coming to resemble the white-collar hell that had so often jostled Lemmon on screen. But there was no workable lesson to be found by Lemmon in any of those past portraits. When life imitates art, artists must finally face life.

Jack Lemmon dropped from public view for nearly nine months. Fans were left to guess whether this absence was simply a gestation period, or the first step to oblivion. Then, an advertisement appeared, first in the *New York Times* and later in other newspapers. It showed a wistful, mustachioed face, in a photograph that was washed out and grainy. An insert picture held the face in resolution, mustache drooping, cigar clenched between set teeth. Lemmon was back.

Few characters could be further from Jack's personal experience than a bailbondsman. But that's what he portrays in *Alex and the Gypsy* (1976) and for all he plays it, Lemmon might have been springing convicts since he was old enough to strike a match. Visually, it is a Lemmon unlike any before, even beyond the charismatic half-vampire, half-harlequin countenance. The old tension has become a throttled passion, and the characteristic alienation is tinged with a guarded loneliness.

The story tells of a dour, sardonic bailbondsman, another of life's hecklers. He has opened his shell only once, and then for a fling with a daffy, conniving young gypsy woman, who leaves him the moment their relationship becomes emotionally parched. When she is later jailed for assault, she contacts Alex and implores him to post her $30,000 bail. He knows that she

INTRODUCING JACK LEMMON

"I am not your run-of-the-mill bailbondsman. I insist on image."—as Alexander Main in *Alex and the Gypsy*, 1976

will skip bail at the first opportunity, just as he knows that a prison term will all but kill her.

Alex springs the Gypsy, and with some exertion manages to keep her under wraps up to the eve of the trial. Without a word, he then lets her slip away, aware that forfeiture will bankrupt him. It is an act of assertion, not submission. For a man who has made a living of others' misfortune, the reasoned gesture of release liberates him as much as it does her. He is broke, but free.

After thirty-three major motion pictures, this is the first time a Jack Lemmon performance has ended in freedom. The film is erratic, and Genevieve Bujold's Gypsy is something beyond eccentric. But Lemmon's Alex is a wide-ranging character that sacrifices no credibility or drive. He is as capable of kindness as he is of killing, but manages to avoid both. He is an interior personality whose real thoughts and emotions break through to his crusty exterior in odd pieces and packages. Alex always knows what he is doing, even if he tends to do too little too late in the way of finishing touches.

*ALEX AND THE GYPSY (1976).
As Alex*

ALEX AND THE GYPSY (1976). With Genevieve Bujold

Alex and the Gypsy did not set the film world on its ear, any more than it inflated the ranks of gypsies and bailbondsmen. But it does place before the movie-going public a Jack Lemmon that is identifiable, and yet unique. It is essentially the same face, if lined and matured, and the same style, if particularized and organic. What's different is the impact, like looking into the face of an old friend and seeing a stranger. Lemmon has at last dared to roll back the technique and protective energy, and has allowed just a fraction of his soul to emerge. For many actors, soul baring is a blind, a diversion that's as traumatic as changing socks. For Lemmon, it is the edge of a quality that has been absent from even his finest film work—mystique. And he only had to pause to find it.

Jack Lemmon will never stop growing; his vitality is his style, trial and error his signature. He will make mistakes, but he will never stop making films. Stars come and go, but actors remain. Jack Lemmon is an actor.

BIBLIOGRAPHY

Baltake, Joe. "Jack Lemmon." *Films in Review*, January, 1970.
Bester, Alfred. "The Antic Arts." *Holiday*, July, 1961.
Davidson, Muriel. "Under the Lemmon Skin." *Ladies Home Journal*, September, 1963.
Deane, Philip. "He Inherited the Mirth." *Photoplay*, September, 1955.
Farr, Felicia. "My Husband." *Good Housekeeping*, April, 1965.
Finlette, Alice. "That Nice Young Family Next Door." *Modern Screen*, October, 1955.
Greenberg, Steven (interviewer). "Jack Lemmon." *Film Comment*, May-June, 1973.
Hale, Wanda. "Lemmon Beat Harvard Purism with 'Thanks.' " *The New York Daily News*, August 14, 1955.
Hamill, Pete. "The Tiger Saved." *The New York Post*, April 3, 1974.
Hubler, Richard G. "Sweet Slice of Lemmon." *Coronet*, October, 1959.
Hyams, Joe. "At Last: A Happy Actor (Maybe)?" *The New York Times*, July 27, 1959.
Jennings, C. Robert. "A Twist of Jack Lemmon." *Coronet*, August, 1966.
Lemmon, Jack. (guest columnist) "The Voice of Broadway." *The New York Journal-American*, July 31, 1960.
Life. "Does Everybody Here Like Jack?" March 22, 1963.
Madsen, Axel. *Billy Wilder*. Bloomington: Indiana University Press, 1969.
Prouse, Derek. "Kotcher in the Rye." *London Sunday Times*, April 23, 1973.
Tornabene, Lyn. "Lunch Date with Jack Lemmon." *Cosmopolitan*, December, 1960.
Widener, Don. *Lemmon*. New York: Macmillan Publishing Company, Inc., 1975.
Wilkie, Jane. "Jack Lemmon." *Modern Screen*, January, 1955.
Wood, Tom. *The Bright Side Of Billy Wilder, Primarily*. Garden City: Doubleday and Co., Inc., 1970.

THE FILMS OF JACK LEMMON

The director's name follows the release date. A (c) following the release date indicates that the film is in color. Sp indicates Screenplay and b/o indicates based/on.

1. IT SHOULD HAPPEN TO YOU. Columbia, 1954. *George Cukor.* Sp: Garson Kanin. Cast: Judy Holliday, Peter Lawford, Michael O'Shea, Connie Gilchrist, Vaughn Taylor, Constance Bennett, Ilka Chase, Wendy Barrie, Melville Cooper.

2. PHFFFT! Columbia, 1954. *Mark Robson.* Sp: George Axelrod. Cast: Judy Holliday, Jack Carson, Kim Novak, Luella Gear, Arny Freeman, Donald Randolph.

3. THREE FOR THE SHOW. Columbia, 1955 (c). *H. C. Potter.* Sp: Edward Hope and Leonard Stern, b/o play by W. Somerset Maugham. Cast: Betty Grable, Marge and Gower Champion, Myron McCormick, Paul Harvey. A musical remake of *Too Many Husbands* (1940).

4. MISTER ROBERTS. Warners, 1955 (c). *John Ford and Mervyn LeRoy.* Sp: Frank Nugent and Joshua Logan, b/o play by Logan and Thomas Heggen. Cast: Henry Fonda, James Cagney, William Powell, Betsy Palmer, Philip Carey, Ward Bond, Nick Adams.

5. MY SISTER EILEEN. Columbia, 1955 (c). *Richard Quine.* Sp: Blake Edwards and Richard Quine, b/o play by Joseph Fields and Jerome Chodorov. Cast: Janet Leigh, Betty Garrett, Robert Fosse, Kurt Kasznar, Richard York, Tommy Rall. A musical remake of *My Sister Eileen* (1942).

6. YOU CAN'T RUN AWAY FROM IT. Columbia, 1956 (c). *Dick Powell.* Sp: Claude Binyon and Robert Riskin, b/o short story by Samuel Hopkins Adams. Cast: June Allyson, Charles Bickford, Jim Backus, Paul Gilbert, Stubby Kaye, Allyn Joslyn, Henny Youngman. A musical remake of *It Happened One Night* (1934).

7. FIRE DOWN BELOW. Columbia, 1957 (c). *Robert Parrish.* Sp: Irwin Shaw, b/o novel by Max Catto. Cast: Rita Hayworth, Robert Mitchum, Herbert Lom, Anthony Newley, Bernard Lee, Bonar Colleano.

8. OPERATION MAD BALL. Columbia, 1957. *Richard Quine.* Sp: Arthur Carter, Jed Harris, and Blake Edwards, b/o play by Carter. Cast: Ernie Kovacs, Kathryn Grant, Mickey Rooney, Dick York, Arthur O'Connell, Jeanne Manet, Roger Smith, James Darren.

9. COWBOY. Columbia, 1958 (c). *Delmer Daves*. Sp: Edmund H. North, b/o Frank Harris's *My Reminiscences as a Cowboy*. Cast: Glenn Ford, Brian Donlevy, Anna Kashfi, Dick York, Victor Manuel Mendoza, Richard Jaeckel.

10. BELL, BOOK AND CANDLE. Columbia, 1958 (c). *Richard Quine*. Sp: Daniel Taradash, b/o play by John Van Druten. Cast: Kim Novak, James Stewart, Ernie Kovacs, Hermione Gingold, Janice Rule, Elsa Lanchester.

11. SOME LIKE IT HOT. United Artists, 1959. *Billy Wilder*. Sp: Billy Wilder and I.A.L. Diamond, b/o story by R. Thoeren and M. Logan. Cast: Marilyn Monroe, Tony Curtis, George Raft, Pat O'Brien, Joe E. Brown, Nehemiah Persoff, Joan Shawlee, Beverly Wills, George E. Stone, Dave Barry.

12. IT HAPPENED TO JANE. Columbia, 1959 (c). *Richard Quine*. Sp: Norman Katkov, b/o story *That Jane From Maine* by Katkov and Max Wilk. Cast: Doris Day, Ernie Kovacs, Steve Forrest, Russ Brown, Parker Fennelly, Mary Wickes, Casey Adams, Walter Greaza.

13. THE APARTMENT. United Artists, 1960. *Billy Wilder*. Sp: Billy Wilder and I.A.L. Diamond. Cast: Shirley MacLaine, Fred MacMurray, Ray Walston, Edie Adams, Hope Holiday, Jack Kruschen, David Lewis, Joan Shawlee, Joyce Jameson.

14. PEPE. Columbia, 1960 (c). *George Sidney*. Sp: Dorothy Kingsley and Claude Binyon, Leonard Spigelgass and Sonya Levien, b/o play by L. Bush-Fekete. Cast: Cantinflas, Dan Dailey, Shirley Jones, Edward G. Robinson, and many guest stars.

15. THE WACKIEST SHIP IN THE ARMY. Columbia, 1961 (c). *Richard Murphy*. Sp: Richard Murphy, Herbert Margolis and William Raynor, b/o story by Herbert Carlson. Cast: Ricky Nelson, John Lund, Tom Tully, Mike Kellin, Chips Rafferty, Patricia Driscoll, Joby Baker.

16. THE NOTORIOUS LANDLADY. Columbia, 1962. *Richard Quine*. Sp: Larry Gelbart and Blake Edwards, b/o short story *The Notorious Tenant* by Margery Sharp. Cast: Kim Novak, Fred Astaire, Lionel Jeffries, Estelle Winwood, Maxwell Reed, Phillipa Bevans, Henry Daniell.

17. DAYS OF WINE AND ROSES. Warners, 1962. *Blake Edwards*. Sp: J. P. Miller, b/o his television play. Cast: Lee Remick, Jack Klugman, Charles Bickford, Alan Hewitt, Jack Albertson, Debbie Megowan.

18. IRMA LA DOUCE. United Artists, 1963 (c). *Billy Wilder*. Sp: Billy Wilder and I.A.L. Diamond, b/o musical play by Marguerite Monnot, Alexandre Breffort, Julian More, David Heneker and Monty Norman. Cast: Shirley MacLaine, Lou Jacobi, Bruce Yarnell, Herschel Bernardi, Hope Holiday, Joan Shawlee.

19. UNDER THE YUM YUM TREE. Columbia, 1963 (c). *David Swift*. Sp: Lawrence Roman and David Swift, b/o play by Roman. Cast: Carol Lynley, Dean Jones, Edie Adams, Paul Lynde, Imogene Coca, Robert Lansing.

20. GOOD NEIGHBOR SAM. Columbia, 1964 (c). *David Swift*. Sp: James Fritzell, Everett Greenbaum and David Swift, b/o novel by Jack Finney. Cast: Romy Schneider, Dorothy Provine, Edward G. Robinson, Michael Connors, Edward Andrews, Louis Nye, Robert Q. Lewis, Joyce Jameson.

21. HOW TO MURDER YOUR WIFE. United Artists, 1965 (c). *Richard Quine*. Sp: George Axelrod. Cast: Virna Lisi, Claire Trevor, Eddie Mayehoff, Terry-Thomas, Mary Wickes, Alan Hewitt, Jack Albertson, Sidney Blackmer, Max Showalter.

22. THE GREAT RACE. Warners, 1965 (c). *Blake Edwards*. Sp: Blake Edwards and Arthur Ross, b/o story by Edwards. Cast: Tony Curtis, Natalie Wood, Keenan Wynn, Peter Falk, Larry Storch, Vivian Vance, Arthur O'Connell, Dorothy Provine.

23. THE FORTUNE COOKIE. United Artists, 1966. *Billy Wilder*. Sp: Billy Wilder and I.A.L. Diamond. Cast: Judi West, Walter Matthau, Ron Rich, Cliff Osmond, Lurene Tuttle, Les Tremayne, Marge Redmond, Maryesther Denver, Ned Glass.

24. LUV. Columbia, 1967 (c). *Clive Donner*. Sp: Elliott Baker, b/o play by Murray Schisgal. Cast: Peter Falk, Elaine May, Nina Wayne, Eddie Mayehoff, Paul Hartman.

25. THE ODD COUPLE. Paramount, 1968 (c). *Gene Saks*. Sp: Neil Simon, b/o his play. Cast: Walter Matthau, Carole Shelley, Monica Evans, Herbert Edelman, John Fiedler, David Sheiner.

26. THE APRIL FOOLS. Cinema Center, 1969 (c). *Stuart Rosenberg*. Sp: Hal Dresner. Cast: Catherine Deneuve, Peter Lawford, Jack Weston, Myrna Loy, Charles Boyer, Sally Kellerman, Harvey Korman.

27. THE OUT-OF-TOWNERS. Paramount, 1970 (c). *Arthur Hiller*. Sp: Neil Simon. Cast: Sandy Dennis, Sandy Baron, Anne Meara, Robert Nichols, Ann Prentiss, Graham Jarvis, Ron Carey.

28. THE WAR BETWEEN MEN AND WOMEN. Cinema Center, 1972 (c). *Melville Shavelson*. Sp: Melville Shavelson and Danny Arnold, suggested by James Thurber's writings and drawings and including "The Last Flower." Cast: Barbara Harris, Jason Robards, Herb Edelman, Lisa Gerritsen, Moosie Drier, Severn Darden, Lisa Eilbacher, Olive Dunbar, Margaret Muse, Dr. Joyce Brothers.

29. AVANTI! United Artists, 1972 (c). *Billy Wilder*. Sp: Billy Wilder and I.A.L. Diamond, b/o play by Samuel Taylor. Cast: Juliet Mills, Clive Revill, Edward Andrews, Gianfranco Barra, Franco Angrisano, Pippo Franco, Giselda Castrini.

30. SAVE THE TIGER. Paramount, 1973 (c). *John G. Avildsen*. Sp: Steve Shagan, b/o his novel. Cast: Jack Gilford, Laurie Heineman, Norman Burton, Patricia Smith, Thayer David, William Hansen, Harvey Jason, Liv Von Linden.

31. THE FRONT PAGE. Universal, 1974 (c). *Billy Wilder*. Sp: Billy Wilder and I.A.L. Diamond, b/o play by Ben Hecht and Charles MacArthur. Cast: Walter Matthau, Carol Burnett, Susan Sarandon, Vincent Gardenia, David Wayne, Allen Garfield, Austin Pendleton, Charles Durning. Previously filmed in 1930 and in 1940 as *His Girl Friday*.

32. THE PRISONER OF SECOND AVENUE. Warners, 1975 (c). *Melvin Frank*. Sp: Neil Simon, b/o his play. Cast: Anne Bancroft, Gene Saks, Elizabeth Wilson, Florence Stanley, Macine Stuart, Edward Peck, Gene Blakely, Ivor Francis, Stack Pierce.

33. ALEX AND THE GYPSY. Twentieth Century-Fox, 1976 (c). *John Korty*. Sp: Lawrence B. Marcus, b/o novella *The Bailbondsman* by Stanley Elkin. Cast: Genevieve Bujold, James Woods, Gino Ardito, Robert Emhardt, Tito Vandis, Bill Cort, Todd Martin.

34. AIRPORT 1977. Universal, 1977 (c). *Jerry Jameson*. Sp: David Spector and Michael Scheff. Cast: James Stewart, Lee Grant, Darren McGavin, Brenda Vaccaro, Olivia de Havilland, Joseph Cotten, George Kennedy, Tom Sullivan.

Directed by Jack Lemmon

KOTCH. Cinerama, 1971 (c). Sp: John Paxton. Cast: Walter Matthau, Deborah Winters, Felicia Farr, Charles Aldman, Ellen Geer.

INDEX

(Italicized page numbers
indicate photographs)

Ad-libbers, The, 29
Albert, Eddie, 29
Albertson, Jack, 24, 26
Alex and the Gypsy, 145, *146*, 147, *147*
Allyson, June, 51-52, *55, 56*
Ameche, Don, 29
Angel Street, 21
Apartment, The, 12, 74, *75*, 76-80, *76, 77, 79, 81*, 93, 130
April Fools, The, 118, 120, *123, 125*
Apron Strings, 26
Arnow, Max, 31
Arrival of Kitty, The, 27
Asro, Alexander, 31
Astaire, Fred, 88, 91, *91*
Astin, Patty Duke, *143*
Avanti!, 125, 127, 130, *132, 133*
Avildsen, John G., 127, 130, 134
Axelrod, George, 42, 106
Ayres, Lew, 11

Baker, Elliott, 115
Bancroft, Anne, 139, 141, *141*, 143
Barrymore, John, 33-34
Behrman, S. N., 85
Bell, Book and Candle, 49, 62-64, *63, 64*
Bernstein, Leonard, 49
Blore, Eric, 108
Bogart, Humphrey, 128
Born Yesterday, 34, 36
Boulle, Pierre, *Face of a Hero*, 80
Boyer, Charles, 118
Brando, Marlon, 118
Brecht, Bertolt, 98
Brighter Day, The, 26
Brown, Joe E., 67, 70, *71*
Bruce, Lenny, 115
Bujold, Genevieve, 145, *147*
Burnett, Carol, *138*
Buttons, Red, 143

Cagney, James, 11, 45, 46, 47, 48, 134
Cantinflas, 82, *86*

Capra, Frank, 51
Carroll, Paul Vincent, 27
Carson, Jack, 41
Carter, Arthur, 54
Carter, Richard, 123
Champion, Gower, *41, 42*, 43
Champion, Marge, 43
Charley's Aunt, 27
Chodorov, Jerome, 49
Christie, Agatha, 87, 88
Cleopatra, 93
Clift, Montgomery, 62
Cline, Richard, 124
Cohn, Harry, 31, 40, 59, 82
Colbert, Claudette, 52
Collingwood, Charles, *28*
Comden, Betty, 49
Cooper, Gladys, *27*
Couple Next Door, The, 29
Coward, Noël, 100
Cowboy, 59-60, *61*, 62
Cukor, George, 31, 35
Curtis, Tony, 65, *66*, 68, *68*, 70, 108, *111*

Dark of the Moon, 26
Darren, James, 57
Daves, Delmer, 62
Day, Doris, 73, *74, 75*, 100
Day Lincoln Was Shot, The, 25
Days of Wine and Roses, 12, *92*, 93-96, *95, 96*
Deneuve, Catherine, 118, *125*
Dennis, Sandy, 121, *128*
Diamond, I. A. L., 73, 74
Dickenson, Don, 26
Doll, Bill, 17
Double Indemnity, 78
Dresner, Hal, 118
Drier, Moosie, *130*
Drunkard, The, 26

East of Eden, 50
Edelman, Herb, 124
Edwards, Blake, 94, 108
Elmer Gantry, 80
Ensign Pulver, 85n

Entertainer, The, *142*, 143-44

Face of a Hero, 80, 82, 96
Falk, Peter, 108, 115
Fanfaren der Liebe (Fanfares of Love), 65
Farr, Felicia (wife), 82, *84*, 97, 124, 134
Fields, Joseph, 49
Fire Down Below, 52-54, *57, 58*
Fonda, Henry, 45, 47, *48*
Ford, Glenn, 59, 60, 62, *62*
Ford, John, 34, 45, 46-47
Forrest, Steve, *74*
Fortune Cookie, The, 108, 111, *113*, 114
Fosse, Bob, 50
Frank, Melvin, 139
Frankenheimer, John, 28
Front Page, The, 134, 138, *138, 139*

Gable, Clark, 51, 52
Garrett, Betty, 49, 50, *51*
Gershwin, George, 43, 45
Gershwin, Ira, 43, 45
Gilbert, Billy, 11
Gilford, Jack, *136*
Gingold, Hermione, 63
Gish, Lillian, *25*
Gold in Them Thar Hills, 17
Good Neighbor Sam, 12, *13*, 102, 104-6, *105, 107*
Grable, Betty, *41, 42*, 43, 45
Grant, Cary, 11, 12, 67, 68, 97, 138
Grant, Kathryn, 57
Great Race, The, 108, *111, 112*
Green, Adolph, 49

Hagen, Uta, 24
Harris, Barbara, 124, *130, 131*
Harris, Frank, *My Reminiscences as a Cowboy*, 59, 60
Hart, Bernard, 29
Hart, Moss, 29
Hawks, Howard, 12, 62, 97, 138
Hayworth, Rita, 12, 52, 54, *57*
Heaven for Betsy, 29
Hecht, Ben, 42
    Front Page, The, 134

Heggen, Thomas, 45
Heston, Charlton, 28
High Sierra, 128
Hiller, Arthur, 121, 139
His Girl Friday, 138
Hitchcock, Alfred, 87, 88
Hoch, Winton, 45
Holliday, Judy, 12, 31, 33, 34-35, *34, 35*, 36, 37, 38, *38*, 40, 41, 42
Howe, James Wong, 63
Howe, Maude DeWolfe, 19
How to Murder Your Wife, 12, 106, 108, *109, 110*

Idiot's Delight, 121
I Remember Mama, 28
Irma La Douce, 97-100, *98, 99, 101*, 127
Irving, Charles, 28
It Happened One Night, 51
It Happened to Jane, 73-74, *74, 75*
It Should Happen to You, *34, 35*, 35-36, 37, 40, 91, 93, 118, 120

Jack Loves Cinnie, 29
John Loves Mary, 26
Johnson, Ben, *143*
Jones, Dean, 102, *104*
Jordan, Eddie, 18
Joseph, Bob, 80

Kaeger, Freddie, 82
Kanin, Garson, 35
Karns, Roscoe, 11
Kasznar, Kurt, *52*
Kellerman, Sally, 118
Kid from Kalamazoo, The, 28
Killiam, Paul, 24
Korman, Harvey, 118
Kotch, 123-24, *129*
Kovacs, Ernie, 59, *60*, 63, *64*, 73-74
Kraft Theater, 27

Lady Windermere's Fan, 26
Lamorisse, Albert, 85
Lancaster, Burt, 80
Lanchester, Elsa, 63, *63, 64*

156

Lang, Charles, Jr., 67
Langford, Frances, 29
Laurie, Piper, 93
Lawford, Peter, 36, 118, *123*
Leigh, Janet, 49, 50, *51*
Lemmon, Christopher (son), 40
Lemmon, Courtney Noel (daughter), 114
Lemmon, John Uhler, Jr. (father), 17, 18, 19, 22, 24, 85, 93, 96, 97
Lemmon, Mildred LaRue Noel (mother), 17, 18, 19, 26, 82, 93, 118
LeRoy, Mervyn, 47
Levene, Sam, 29
Lilies of the Field, 96
Lisi, Virna, 12, 108, *110*
Logan, Joshua, 45
Long Gray Line, The, 34, 35
Loy, Myrna, 118
Lumet, Sidney, 28
Lupino, Ida, *23*
Luv, 115, *116, 119*
Lynley, Carol, 12, 102, *104*
Lynn, Diana, 31

MacArthur, Charles, *Front Page, The*, 134
McCormick, Myron, 45
McCullough, Andy, 24
McDowall, Roddy, 21
McKenney, Ruth, 49
MacLaine, Shirley, 12, *77*, 78, 98, *98*, *99*, 100
MacMurray, Fred, 78, *79*
Malden, Karl, *143*
Mandelbaum, Mitzi, 24
March, Fredric, 123
Marriageable Male, *23*
Marshall, Herbert, *27*
Marx Brothers, 29
Massey, Raymond, *25*
Matthau, Walter, 111, *113*, 114, 117, *120*, *122*, 123, *129*, 134, 138, *139*, *143*
Maugham, W. Somerset, 43
May Elaine, 115, *119*
Miller, J. P., 93
Mills, Hayley, 100
Mills, Juliet, 125, 127, *132, 133*

Miner, Worthington, 27
Minnelli, Vincente, 51
Mister Roberts, 44, 45-48, *46, 48, 50*
Mitchum, Robert, 52, 53, 54, *58*
Monash, Paul, 138
Monroe, Marilyn, 12, 65, 67, 68, *69*
Mulligan, Gerry, 115
My Sister Eileen, 10, 49-50, *51, 53*
Mystery of 13, The, 27

Name for Herself, A, 34
Nelson, Ricky, 85, *87*
Nichols, Mike, 115
Nicholson, Jack, 134
Notorious, 87
Notorious Landlady, The, 87-88, *90*, 91, *91*, 93
Novak, Kim, 12, *38, 39*, 41, 63, *63*, 64, 88, 90, 91, *91*

O'Brien, Edmond, *50*
O'Brien, Margaret, *27*
O'Brien, Pat, 67
O'Connell, Arthur, 57, 59
Odd Couple, The, 115, 117, *120, 122*
Olivier, Laurence, *143*
Operation Mad Ball, 54, 57, 59, *59*, 60
Orry-Kelly, 68
Osborne, John, *Entertainer, The*, 143-44
Out-of-Towners, The, 121, *126, 128*, 138, 139

Pacino, Al, 134
Parrish, Robert, 54
Parsons, Estelle, 19
Penn, Arthur, 28
Pepe, 82, 85, *86*
Person to Person, 28
Phffft!, 31, *32, 38, 39*, 40-42
Playboy of the Western World, The, 19
Playhouse 90, *27*, 80
Powell, Dick, 51, 52
Powell, William, 45, *46*, 47
Power, Tyrone, 45
Power of Darkness, The, 24, 26
Prisoner of Second Avenue, The, 138-39, *140*, 141, *141*, 143

Provine, Dorothy, 105, *105*

Quine, Richard, 50, 54, 57, 63, 73, 87, 88, 91, 97, 100, 106

Raft, George, 67
Red Balloon, The, 85
Redford, Robert, 134
Red River, 62
Remick, Lee, *92*, 94, 95, *96*
Rich, Ron, *113*
Road of Life, 26
Robards, Jason, Jr., 124
Robert Montgomery Presents, 28, 31
Robertson, Cliff, 93
Robin, Leo, 49
Rogers, Ginger, *143*
Roman, Lawrence, 100, 102
Room Service, 29, 31, 33, 50-51
Rooney, Mickey, 59, *59*, 85
Russell, Harold, *143*
Russell, Rosalind, 49, 138

Saint, Eva Marie, 28, *50*, *143*
Saks, Gene, 117
Save the Tiger, 14, 127-28, 130, 135, *136*, *137*
Scarface, 67
Schell, Maximilian, *143*
Schisgal, Murray, *Luv*, 115
Schneider, Romy, 105, *105*, *107*
Shagan, Steve, *Save the Tiger*, 127-28, 130
Shavelson, Melville, 124
Shaw, Irwin, 54
Shea, Maury, 22, 24
Sherwood, Robert, *Idiot's Delight*, 121
Simon, Neil, 12
   Odd Couple, The, 115, 117
   Out-of-Towners, The, 121, 138
   Prisoner of Second Avenue, The, 138-139, 141
Sloane, Everett, 31
Slocum, Brooks, 17
Smith, Roger, 57
Some Like It Hot, 12, 65-71, *66*, *68*, *69*, *71*, 114

Squire, Katherine, *96*
Stalag 17, 48
Steiger, Rod, 28, *143*
Stewart, James, 62-63, *64*
Stone, Cynthia (wife), 26, 28, 29, 33, 40, 49, 93
Stowaway in the Sky, 85, 87
Studio One, 28
Styne, Jule, 49
Swift, David, 100, 102, 104, 105
Synge, John Millington, 19

Taylor, Samuel, 125
Terry-Thomas, 108
That Wonderful Guy, 28
Thoeren (German writer), 65
Three for the Show, *41*, *42*, 43, 45
Three Men on a Horse, 26
Thurber, James, 124
Tolstoy, Leo, 24, 26
Too Many Husbands, 43
Topkins, Katherine, 123
Trevor, Claire, 108, *143*

Under the Yum-Yum Tree, 12, 97, 100, 102, *103*, *104*
Ustinov, Peter, *143*

Van Druten, John, 21, 62
Van Fleet, Jo, *50*

Wackiest Ship in the Army, The, 85, *87*, *89*
Walker, Robert, 11, 85n
War Between Men and Women, The, 124, *130*, *131*
Warner, Jack, 93
Wayne, David, 48
Wayne, John, 62
Welles, Orson, 73
Weston, Jack, 118
Widener, Don, "Slow Guillotine, The," 121
Wilde, Oscar, 26
Wilder, Billy, 12, 15, 42, 47-48, 65, 70, 73, 74, 78, 80, 94, 97, 98, *98*, 100, 108, 114, 125, 127, 130, 134, 138
Winters, Ralph, 124

Winters, Shelley, *143*
Winwood, Estelle, *91*
Wonderful Town, 49
Wood, Natalie, 108, *111*

York, Dick, 57, *59*
You Bet Your Life, 33n
You Can't Run Away From It, 50-52, *55*, *56*
Young Woodley, 21

ABOUT THE AUTHOR
Will Holtzman has lectured on film at Wesleyan University, in Middletown, Connecticut and has written for the *St. Louis Globe-Democrat, The Real Paper, The Journal of Popular Film*, and the Film Department of the Wadsworth Atheneum. He is author of *William Holden*, a volume in the Pyramid Illustrated History of the Movies.

ABOUT THE EDITOR
Ted Sennett is the author of *Warner Brothers Presents*, a tribute to the great Warners films of the thirties and forties, and of *Lunatics and Lovers*, on the long-vanished but well-remembered "screwball" movie comedies of the past. The editor of *Bijou: The Magazine of the Movies*, he also edited *The Movie Buff's Book, The Movie Buff's Book 2*, and *The Old-Time Radio Book*. He lives in New Jersey with his wife and three children.